Native Americans
of the Northwest Coast

BIBLIOGRAPHICAL SERIES
The Newberry Library Center
for the History of the American Indian

General Editor
Francis Jennings
Assistant Editor
William R. Swagerty

The Center Is Supported by Grants from
The National Endowment for the Humanities
The Ford Foundation
The W. Clement and Jessie V. Stone Foundation
The Woods Charitable Fund, Inc.
Mr. Gaylord Donnelley

Native Americans of the Northwest Coast

A Critical Bibliography

ROBERT STEVEN GRUMET

Published for the Newberry Library

Indiana University Press

BLOOMINGTON AND LONDON

Manufactured in the United States of America

Library of Congress Cataloging in Publication Data

Grumet, Robert Steven.
    Native Americans of the northwest coast.

    (Bibliographical series—The Newberry Library Center for the History of the American Indian)
    Includes indexes.
    1. Indians of North America—Northwest coast of North America—Bibliography. I. Title. II. Series: Bibliographical series.
Z1209.2.N67G78 [E78.N78] 016.9795′004′97 79-2165
ISBN 0–253–30385–0 pbk.   1 2 3 4 5 83 82 81 80 79

CONTENTS

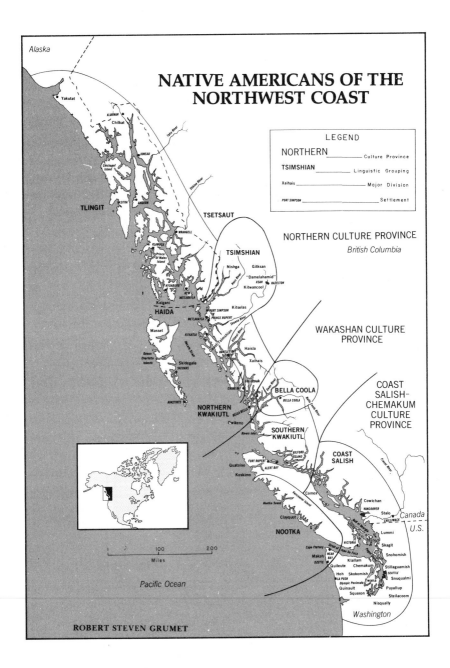

NATIVE AMERICANS OF THE NORTHWEST COAST

Alaska

LEGEND

NORTHERN _____ Culture Province

TSIMSHIAN _____ Linguistic Grouping

Xaihais _____ Major Division

PORT SIMPSON _____ Settlement

NORTHERN CULTURE PROVINCE
British Columbia

WAKASHAN CULTURE PROVINCE

COAST SALISH-CHEMAKUM CULTURE PROVINCE

Yakutat

KLUKWAN
Chilkat

JUNEAU

Chichagof
Island

SITKA ANGOON

TLINGIT

WRANGELL

KLAWOCK
Prince
Of Wales
Island

HYDABURG
NEW
METLAKATLA

Kaigani

HAIDA

Masset

Queen
Charlotte
Islands

Skidegale
SKIDANS

NINSTINTS

TSETSAUT

TSIMSHIAN

Nishga   Gitksan

"Damelahamid"
KSAN HAZELTON
Kitwancool

Kitselas

PORT SIMPSON
METLAKATLA *PRINCE RUPERT*
KITKATLA

HARTLEY BAY   Haisla

Xaihais

Heiltsuk

CHINA HAT

NORTHERN KWAKIUTL

BELLA BELLA

BELLA COOLA

BELLA COOLA

Owikeno

Rivers Inlet

SOUTHERN KWAKIUTL

GILFORD
ISLAND

Quatsino   FORT RUPERT

Koskimo   ALERT BAY

COAST SALISH

Comox

Cowichan

VANCOUVER

Stalo
CHILLIWACK

Clayoquot

NOOTKA

Lummi

VICTORIA

Cape Flattery
Makah   NEAH
BAY
OZETTE   Klallam   Skagit

Quileute   Chemakum   Snohomish

Hoh   Skokomish   Stillaguamish
LA PUSH   *SEATTLE*
Olympic Peninsula   Snuqualmi
Quinault   Squaxon   Puyallup
Steilacoom

Nisqually

Washington

Pacific Ocean

100   200
Miles

Canada
U.S.

ROBERT STEVEN GRUMET

AUTHOR'S PREFACE

The native cultures of the Northwest Coast of North America have attracted considerable attention since the European discovery of the region in 1741. The long cedar canoes, the plank house villages with their sinuous pickets of crest poles, the extravagances of the potlatch, and the majesty and genius of their art have long captured the imagination of the world. Because of this interest, several thousand books, monographs, and articles have been devoted to the aboriginal peoples of the North Pacific Coast. A substantial portion of this literature has been listed in volume 3 of the 4th edition of the *Ethnographic Bibliography of North America* [152]. Specialized bibliographies have also appeared in *British Columbia Studies, Northwest Anthropological Research Notes,* and the *Oregon Historical Quarterly.* No effort, however, has been made to annotate or otherwise evaluate the materials contained in these collections. It is therefore the purpose of this volume to distill this massive documentation into a brief evaluative bibliography of both the best and the most readily available reports of Northwest Coast ethnography.

Definition of the Northwest Coast culture area has depended upon the particular perspective of each author. At the maximum, the culture area has been taken to include the whole of the northwest Pacific rim from southwestern Alaska to coastal California; as a minimum, authors have focused upon the "classic" North Coast cultures of southeastern Alaska and northern British Columbia. The area outlined by the *Ethnographic Bibliography of North America,* stretching from the "the southeastern Alaskan Panhandle and the coast of British Columbia to the southern end of Puget Sound in northwestern Washington," has been adopted for this volume. This area includes all the major Northwest Coast cultures recognized by scholars and other writers. It does not include those societies on the borders of the region that possess many, but not all, of the attributes traditionally ascribed to Northwest Coast culture. Listings of many of these culture traits may be found in Philip Drucker's "Culture Element Distribution Number 26: Northwest Coast" [67] and his more accessible "Sources of Northwest Coast Culture" [70].

This essay is a narrative bibliography of the major publications of Northwest Coast archaeology, ethnohistory, and ethnography. It excludes many other topics traditionally associated with Northwest Coast studies, such as myths, texts, languages, and physical anthropology. Purely historical tracts and highly specialized research papers have also been excluded. Information on myths and legends may be found in the publications of the American Folklore Society, the American Antiquarian and Oriental Society, the United States Bureau of American Ethnology, and the Canadian National Museum of Man. Text materials have frequently appeared in the *Columbia University Contributions to Anthropology,* the *University of Washington Publications in An-*

thropology, Memoirs of the American Museum of Natural History, and the *Annual Reports of the Bureau of American Ethnology.* Many papers on Northwest Coast linguistics are contained in the *International Journal of American Linguistics, American Linguistics,* and *Language.* Articles devoted to physical anthropology may be found in the *American Anthropologist* and the *American Journal of Physical Anthropology.* Many historical articles have appeared in the *Indian Historian,* the *Oregon Historical Quarterly,* the *Pacific Northwest Quarterly* (formerly the *Washington Historical Quarterly*), the *British Columbia Historical Quarterly,* and the *American West.* The following journals have published many articles of specialized interest:

American Anthropologist, Washington, D.C.
Arctic Anthropology, Madison, Wisconsin
The Beaver, Winnipeg, Manitoba, Canada
B.C. Studies, Vancouver, British Columbia, Canada
Bulletin of the National Museum of Canada, Ottawa,
    Ontario, Canada
Davidson Journal of Anthropology, Seattle, Washington
Economic Botany, The Bronx, New York
Ethnohistory, Tucson, Arizona
Ethnology, Pittsburgh, Pennsylvania
Human Organization, New York, New York
Journal of Ethnological Theory (formerly the *Southwestern
    Journal of Anthropology*), Albuquerque, New Mexico
*Journal of the Royal Anthropological Institute of Great
    Britian and Ireland,* London, England
Natural History, New York, New York

Northwest Anthropological Research Notes, Moscow,
   Idaho
*Proceedings and Transactions of the Royal Society of
   Canada*, Montreal, Quebec, Canada
*Report of the British Association for the Advancement of
   Science*, London, England
Syesis (successor to various serials published by the
   Provincial Museum of British Columbia), Victoria,
   British Columbia, Canada
Western Canadian Journal of Anthropology, Edmonton,
   Alberta, Canada

Archives and Libraries Containing Significant Collections
of Northwest Coast
Manuscripts and Publications

Americana Room, New York Public Library, New York
Bancroft Library, University of California, Berkeley
British Columbia Indian Language Project, Victoria
British Museum, London, England
Huntington Free Library, Museum of the American
   Indian, Heye Foundation, Bronx, New York
The Huntington Library, San Marino, California
Library of the American Museum of Natural History,
   New York
Library of the American Philosophical Society,
   Philadelphia, Pennsylvania
Library of the University of British Columbia,
   Vancouver

Museum of Culture History, University of California,
  Los Angeles
Museo National, Madrid, Spain
National Anthropological Archives, Smithsonian
  Institution, Washington, D.C.
National Museum of Man, Ottawa, Ontario, Canada
Northwest Collection, Library of the University of
  Washington, Seattle
Provincial Library of British Columbia, Victoria

Museums Containing Significant Collections of Northwest Coast Artifacts

Alaska State Museum, Juneau
American Museum of Natural History, New York
British Columbia Provincial Museum, Victoria
British Museum, London, England
Brooklyn Museum, Brooklyn, New York
Centennial Museum, Vancouver, British Columbia
Cranbrook Institute of Science, Bloomfield Hills,
  Michigan
Denver Art Museum, Denver, Colorado
Field Museum of Natural History, Chicago, Illinois
Lowie Museum of Anthropology, University of
  California, Berkeley
Milwaukee Public Museum, Milwaukee, Wisconsin
Musée L'Homme, Paris, France
Museum of the American Indian, Heye Foundation,
  New York

Museum of Anthropology, University of British
    Columbia, Vancouver
Museum of Anthropology and Ethnography of the
    Academy of Sciences, Leningrad, Soviet Union
Museum of Northern British Columbia, Prince Rupert
Museum of Primitive Art, New York
National Museum of Man, National Museums of
    Canada, Ottawa, Ontario
National Museum of Natural History, Smithsonian
    Institution, Washington, D.C.
Nelson Art Gallery, Kansas City, Missouri
Peabody Museum of Archaeology and Ethnology,
    Harvard University, Cambridge, Massachusetts
Portland Art Museum, Portland, Oregon
Royal Ontario Museum, Toronto
Thomas Burke Memorial Washington State Museum,
    Seattle
University Museum, University of Pennsylvania,
    Philadelphia
Whatcom Museum of History and Art, Bellingham,
    Washington

RECOMMENDED WORKS

For the Beginner

[10]   Charles Marius Barbeau, *Totem Poles.*

[69]   Philip Drucker, *Indians of the Northwest Coast.*

[72]   Philip Drucker, *Cultures of the North Pacific Coast.*

[76]   Wilson Duff, *The Indian History of British Columbia.*

[134]   Forrest E. La Violette, *The Struggle for Survival.*

[142]   Thomas R. McFeat, ed., *Indians of the North Pacific Coast.*

For a Basic Library Collection

[15]   Homer Garner Barnett, *The Coast Salish of British Columbia.*

[20]   Franz Boas, *The Social Organization and Secret Societies of the Kwakiutl Indians.*

[22]   Franz Boas, *Tsimshian Mythology.*

[36]   Helen Codere, *Fighting with Property.*

[44]   Elizabeth Colson, *The Makah Indians.*

[50]   Edward Sheriff Curtis, *The Kwakiutl.*

[58]   Frederica De Laguna, *Under Mount Saint Elias.*

[68]   Philip Drucker, *The Northern and Central Nootkan Tribes.*

[71]   Philip Drucker, *The Native Brotherhoods.*

[84]   William W. Elmendorf, *The Structure of Twana Culture.*

[99]   Viola Edmundson Garfield and Paul Stover Wingert, *The Tsimshian Indians and Their Arts.*

[106]   Erna Gunther, *Art in the Life of the Northwest Coast Indian.*

[107]   Erna Gunther, *Indian Life on the Northwest Coast of North America.*

BIBLIOGRAPHICAL ESSAY

Introduction

The cultures of the Northwest Coast are organized into three culture provinces in this volume. The first is the Northern culture province, home of the matrilineal North Coast Tlingit, Haida, Tsimshian, and Northern Kwakiutl-speaking groups. The Northern culture province is often regarded as the climax of Northwest Coast culture. Many of the most impressive elaborations of the secret societies, the crest systems, Northwest Coast art, and other culture traits occurred in this region. The Northern culture province contains three major ecological zones: the coastal, island, and river valley zones. The coastal area is a heavily indented, fiord-sliced region where steep mountains and cliffs border the seas and the protected waters. Scantily forested, with nearly impenetrable backlands, its settlements are restricted to the few narrow stretches of beachfront along sheltered bays and harbors. The Tlingit and Coast Tsimshian primarily make their homes in this zone.

Thousands of islands, many the submerged tips of drowned mountains, shield this rugged coastline from the weather that constantly blows in from the west. These islands, including the large Chichagof and Prince of Wales archipelagoes of Alaska and the Queen Charlotte Islands of British Columbia, are heavily forested with the largest stands of red cedar found along the Coast. Halibut, salmon, and sea mammals frequent this island zone in massive numbers, and the many sheltered locations for settlement on the lee sides of islands insured the presence of many villages during traditional times. Many Tlingit groups inhabit the island zone of southeastern Alaska, with the Haida residing in the Queen Charlottes and the lower Prince of Wales Islands.

Long river systems cut their way to the coast from deep in the interior. Favored with the enormous spawning migrations of salmon and eulachon, or candlefish, the mild riverine environment also offers luxuriant forests and berrying grounds. A further bonus is that there are many days of sunlight along the upper reaches of the rivers, in sharp contrast to the often gloomy conditions along the "rain coast." Many Tlingit live along the lower reaches of the Taku and Stikine rivers. The Tsimshian-speaking Nishga cluster around the eulachon beaches and salmon-spawning grounds of the Nass River. Farther south, the Tsimshian-speaking Gitksan name themselves "People of the Skeena" to honor their river, a major communications route into the interior. The Northern Kwakiutl inhabit the neighboring Kitimat River system.

The Wakashan culture province also consists of three major ecosystems. The Southern Kwakiutl and Salish-speaking Bella Coola inhabit many of the sheltered inlets that serrate the coast between the Queen Charlotte Islands and Vancouver Island. A large number of these deep channels extend well out into a coastal basin somewhat wider than that found to the north. The Bella Coola inhabit a particularly salubrious setting between the Bella Coola and Dean rivers. The bulk of the Southern Kwakiutl groups live in villages scattered throughout the many islands, bays, and inlets of their sea-channel environment, wedged between the mainland and Vancouver Island. The Kwakiutl-speaking Quatsino and Koskimo groups share the outer coast beach and bay environment with the more southerly Nootka. Speakers of the Nootkan language were the only people along the Coast to hunt whales from their large open dugout canoes.

The massive Coast Mountains recede from the shore as one moves south. The Coast Salish-Chemakum culture province is characteristically a land of broad forests, expansive prairies containing camas bulb groves and many types of berries, and placid sounds, bays, and straits flecked with hundreds of islands. The massive Fraser River, with its legendary runs of salmon, piles up the teeming wetland of the Fraser delta where it empties into the Strait of Georgia at Vancouver. The most southerly Quinault group inhabits the damp outer coast reaches below the Nootkan-speaking Makah along the west shore of the Olympic Peninsula of Washington. The northernmost Comox in their turn live as sociocultural and environmental cousins to the sea-channel-dwelling Southern Kwakiutl.

These diverse environmental, linguistic, and sociopolitical settings are nevertheless united by strong similarities. All Northwest Coast groups face the sea, which gives life to the people of its shores. Among the finest woodworkers in the world, their woodcrafting technology and sculptural art styles set them apart from any other peoples. Their highly stratified and class-conscious social structures are not found among other North American maritime hunting and gathering groups. No other peoples possess the complex secret societies, winter ceremonials, Guardian Spirit dances, potlatches, and shamanistic spectacles that have alternately fascinated and appalled outlanders. The Northwest Coast, separated from the rest of North America by unending chains of towering mountains and by a multitude of socioculturally singular institutions, can truly be defined as a discrete region by almost every measure.

General Works

The two best general introductions to the native cultures of the Northwest Coast have been published as successive handbooks for the North Pacific Coast collection of the American Museum of Natural History. The first was published by Pliny Earle Goddard in 1924 [101]. Entitled *Indians of the Northwest Coast,* this scholarly and profusely illustrated classic has been repeatedly reissued with only minor revisions. In its most recent incarnation, Della Kew has added a large selection of photographs in a larger format [128].

The museum published Philip Drucker's *Indians of the Northwest Coast* in 1955 [69] as the successor to Goddard's handbook. This brilliant monograph remains the most comprehensive study of Northwest Coast culture. At once encyclopedic and concise, it presents a well-considered overview of Northwest Coast society and culture. The brief summary chapter synopsizes Drucker's findings as published in his "Sources of Northwest Coast Culture" [70].

An exceptionally wide selection of excerpts from key sources can be found in Thomas McFeat's *Indians of the North Pacific Coast* [142].

A large number of general works devoted to various aspects of Northwest Coast life have been published. Frances Densmore gathered some eighty-three songs from individuals from many coastal groups at the hop-picking grounds at Chilliwack, British Columbia, in 1926. Published in 1943 as *Music of the Indians of British Columbia,* the collection analyzes each song and includes large amounts of related data [61]. Nancy Turner's *Food Plants of British Columbia Indians: Part 1. Coastal Peoples* is an impressively documented and sumptuously illustrated ethnobotanical guidebook based upon published sources and original fieldwork [205]. This low-priced handbook is almost unavailable in the United States, but copies may be obtained from the British Columbia Provincial Museum in Victoria.

Equally impressive, and far more widely available, is Hilary Stewart's *Indian Fishing: Early Methods on the Northwest Coast* [188]. Well documented and magnificently illustrated, this volume examines every major harvesting, processing, and ritual technique practiced along the Coast. Erna Gunther's *A Further Analysis of the First Salmon Ceremony* traces the distribution of this ceremonial complex throughout the Northwest Coast [105].

The finest general study of the dugout canoe technology of the region is Bill Durham's *Indian Canoes of the Northwest Coast* [81]. Well researched from published sources, it provides line drawings and photographs of the many canoe types found along the Coast. Another fine book on Northwest Coast material culture is Hilary Stewart's *Artifacts of the Northwest Coast Indians* [187]. Extensively illustrated and comprehensive, this volume is the best introduction to the many tool types of the Coast.

An excellent popular introduction to Northwest Coast culture is Philip Drucker's *Cultures of the North Pacific Coast* [72]. Agreeably written, with a number of photographs, many in color, it includes accounts of the Tsimshian and Nootka groups and a review of the acculturation history of Indian–European contact in Alaska and British Columbia. Drucker defines acculturation as the cultural processes and the psychological factors that cause and are caused by culture change. His measure of acculturation has, however, tended to be the extent to which native cultures have come to resemble those of the dominant culture.

Children of the Raven, by H. R. Hays, combines an excellent narrative history of the region with a competent description of traditional Northwest Coast culture and an exceptionally valuable account of current events based upon Hays's own field research in Alaska and British Columbia [115]. The book is marred, however, by a substantial number of typographical errors. Another drawback is Hays's unfortunate outmoded culture-and-personality explanation of Northwest Coast society as possessing a "shame-prestige culture."

Emily Carr's *Klee Wyck* is a collection of short stories recalling her early journeys to the abandoned villages and quiet native settlements of the coast of British Columbia at the turn of this century [31]. Intent upon painting scenes of the fast-vanishing native way of life, Carr's reminiscences constitute a remarkable sensory document, evoking the sights, sounds, and smells of the Northwest Coast.

Indian Primitive, by Ralph W. Andrews, presents more than 180 photographs of traditional Northwest Coast life from Alaska to northern California [3]. An unpretentious popular book, its frequent naiveté can be overlooked because of its many fine photographs. It is more difficult to make allowances for the often pedantic tone and numerous misinterpretations contained in *Totem Pole Indians* [218]. Written by the hobbyist Joseph Wherry in 1964, this copiously illustrated volume does provide a rare tourist's-eye view of native life along the Coast during the late 1950s.

Vinson Brown's *Peoples of the Sea Wind* [29] is a handsomely written selection of short stories and brief, derivative ethnographic accounts of traditional native life along the Pacific coast from southwestern Alaska to lower California. The Northwest Coast section of the volume focuses upon the Tlingit, Tsimshian, Kwakiutl, and Nootka groups.

More conventional in format, but far less satisfactory overall, is George Woodcock's *Peoples of the Coast* [222], an ostensibly scientific volume that opens with references to "the megalomaniac concern with prestige" and the "linguistic and political chaos" supposedly characterizing traditional Northwest Coast life. This remarkably uneven study combines cogent discussions of the latest data with alarming inadequacies. Woodcock's presentation of Northwest Coast archaeology and cultural development is the best in any general publication, but he tends to reduce to givens such controversial issues as the alleged Siberian origin of Northwest Coast shamanism.

Brief mention should also be made of the dated, but still widely available, *Introduction to Our Native Peoples,* by A. F. Flucke and A. E. Pickford. This was the first of the British Columbia Heritage series published during the 1960s [92].

The Archaeology of the Region

The Northwest Coast was long regarded as the terra incognita of North American prehistory. A hiatus of more than forty years separated the first investigations that Harlan Ingersoll Smith and Charles Hill-Tout conducted in the greater Vancouver area at the turn of this century from the first modern scientific excavations during the late 1940s. The impenetrable rain forests and thin rocky soils of the Coast were regarded as infertile grounds for archaeological inquiry. Indeed, the only professional archaeological project carried out between the two world wars was Philip Drucker's 1938 site survey of the Northern culture province [66]. The large number of sites located during this survey enabled Drucker to develop the first and only descriptive classification of Northwest Coast artifacts.

The years immediately after World War II saw a resurgence in archaeological activity along the Coast. Most of this work was conducted in the familiar greater Vancouver area. Frederica de Laguna and her associates, however, elected to work on Tlingit archaeology and ethnology in the northern portion of the southeastern Alaska panhandle. De Laguna has described her excavations in the Tlingit communities of Angoon [57] and Yakutat [59] between 1949 and 1952. These excavations were coordinated with ethnographic and ethnohistorical research. The result was the first reconstruction of a historical Northwest Coast culture capable of testing and expanding both the memories of native informants and scanty observations of European explorers.

The late 1960s witnessed an explosion of archaeological activity. The investigations of Charles Borden [26, 27] and Knut Fladmark [89] pushed back the record of human habitation along the Coast some ten thousand years. Borden's activities centered mainly on the greater Vancouver area. Fladmark presented the first paleoecological model of Northwest Coast prehistory. Restricting his findings to the Northern culture province, he traced the Coastal resource base, the prehistoric environment, ethnographic subsistence patterns, and the archaeological record back some five thousand years.

Jerome Cybulski has been involved in Northwest Coast physical anthropology. Using a number of measuring techniques, he found that the craniums of the Coast Salish, Nootka, and Kwakiutl represented a common population, distinct from the Haida of the Queen Charlotte Islands, the other component of his sample [53]. He thus demonstrated that proximity was more important than language in determining physical homogeneity. Cybulski has also published an anthropological description of the physical characteristics of the bodies recovered from the Gust Island burial shelter site on Graham Island, one of the Queen Charlotte Islands [52].

The first survey devoted to recent developments in Northwest Coast archaeology was published as a special issue of *British Columbia Studies* entitled *Archaeology in British Columbia: New Discoveries* [30]. Among the articles in this symposium volume were Roy Carlson's history of British Columbia archaeology; Charles Borden's outline of the culture history of the greater Vancouver area; site and survey reports from the Queen Charlotte Islands, Bella Coola, Vancouver Island, and the Gulf of Georgia, and an excellent bibliography compiled by Knut Fladmark.

Donald Mitchell published his findings from the Montague Harbour midden site (excavated between 1964 and 1968) in *Archaeology of the Gulf of Georgia Area* [148]. He established the area as a distinct environmental, archaeological, and ethnographic entity, reviewed the literature mentioned above, and presented a radiocarbon-dated time sequence of continuous occupation from 1,200 B.C. to A.D. 1,200.

George MacDonald's salvage excavations of three sites on the Queen Charlotte Islands during 1966 and 1967 are reported in *Haida Burial Practices: Three Archaeological Examples* [140]. The data recovered from these sites have permitted archaeological verification of the scanty documentation concerning Haida mortuary practices.

Bjorn Simonsen's *Archaeological Investigations in the Hecate Strait–Milbanke Sound Area of British Columbia* surveys the region as of the summer of 1969 [177]. Simonsen recorded 108 sites in the area and excavated a midden, the Grant Anchorage site. This site revealed a continuous occupation beginning 3,500 years earlier and ending in 1865.

The most exciting development in Northwest Coast archaeology has been the discovery of a number of water-saturated or "wet" sites in British Columbia and Washington. Wet sites, which have been known only since 1970, exist in waterlogged soils below the water table where the lack of oxygen prevents the decay of vegetal substances. The first and most impressive of these sites to be excavated is the Ozette site. Situated on Capa Alava on the Pacific shore of the Olympic Peninsula of Washington, it consists of the remains of at least five plank houses covered by a mud slide some five hundred years ago. Excavators have recovered several thousand wood and basketry artifacts, perfectly preserved. The Makah, whose ancestors inhabited Ozette, have taken part in its excavation and will retain possession of every artifact from the site. They are currently preparing a museum at Neah Bay for the collection and are arranging to train a number of their people at the University of Washington to act as curators.

Because excavations are still in progress, little has been published about the Ozette site. A brief popular account of Ozette may be found in Ruth Kirk and Richard Daugherty, *Hunters of the Whale* [129]. A brief introductory article has been published in Dale Croes, ed., *The Excavation of Water-Saturated Archaeological Sites (Wet Sites) on the Northwest Coast of North America* [46]. This symposium volume also contains reports on ten other wet sites along the Coast, including an article on George MacDonald's and Richard Inglis's key Prince Rupert site in northern British Columbia. The final article deals with wood conservation methods from Europe, with suggestions on their possible application to wet-site archaeology on the Northwest Coast. Scholarly reports on many aspects of the work at Ozette and Prince Rupert are currently in preparation.

The prehistoric rock carving of the Northwest Coast should also be mentioned. Both Edward Meade's *Indian Rock Carvings of the Pacific Northwest* [146] and Beth and Ray Hill's *Indian Petroglyphs of the Pacific*

Northwest [116] are excellent and very well illustrated introductions to the poorly understood pecked carvings on the rocks and cliff sides of many locales in Alaska, British Columbia, and Washington. *Images Stone B.C.*, by the late Wilson Duff [77], is a sumptuous guide to 136 freestanding stone sculptures from throughout the British Columbia coast and the Fraser River valley. It is particularly noteworthy for Duff's analysis of the meanings, "imagings," of these sculptures.

The History of the Region

The best review of the history of European contact with the native populations of the Northwest Coast remains Wilson Duff's *The Indian History of British Columbia* [76]. Though describing only events in British Columbia, including those concerning the interior Salish and Athapaskan groups, it comments on the classification of native groups, their populations, the fur trade and colonial periods, the development of Indian administration, and changes in material culture and religion. Many clear maps and tables trace changes in native political organization and population between the mid-nineteenth century and 1963.

There remains a continuing need to update and extend the scope of Duff's study. The historical portion of H. R. Hays's *Children of the Raven* [115] comes close to filling this need, but it lacks the detail necessary for a comprehensive introduction. Another fine study is Polly and Leon Miller's *The Lost Heritage of Alaska*

[147]. Popularly written, well illustrated, and sufficiently documented, this volume is restricted to southeastern Alaska.

The finest account of the history of eighteenth-century European exploration and trade along the Coast is Erna Gunther's *Indian Life on the Northwest Coast of North America* [107]. Exhaustively documented from manuscript materials and artifacts gathered from many North American and European repositories, it thoroughly reconstructs eighteenth-century Northwest Coast culture. It includes two appendixes on the artifacts collected during eighteenth-century European expeditions.

Joyce Wike's still unpublished doctoral dissertation, "The Effect of the Maritime Fur Trade on Northwest Coast Indian Society" [219], analyzes the consequences of late eighteenth and early nineteenth century seaborne commerce upon native cultures throughout the Coast. Wike stresses the few negative and many beneficial effects of the maritime fur trade, a perspective sometimes overlooked in other studies. Julia Averkieva's *Slavery among the Indians of North America* [7], though difficult to obtain, traces the peculiar institution on the Northwest Coast from its precontact origins to the elaborations of the historical period.

The first modern anthropological field trips to the Coast are reported in Jacobsen's *Alaskan Voyage, 1881–1883* [120] and Rohner's *The Ethnography of Franz Boas* [169]. Jacobsen's account, recently translated from the German by Erna Gunther, records his experience while collecting artifacts among the Kwakiutl, Nootka, and Haida. Rohner compiled pioneer anthropologist Franz Boas's diaries and letters from his field trips to the Coast, conducted between 1886 and 1931. Boas's field researches among the Kwakiutl and Tsimshian stimulated world interest in the Northwest Coast and influenced the manner in which future fieldwork would be conducted by anthropologists in other areas of the world. Mainly gathered from the Boas manuscripts in the American Philosophical Society library in Philadelphia, the materials are supplemented by an excellent discussion of Boas's role in the development of North American anthropology. A chronology of his life and a map of the Coast locations he visited are also included.

The almost century-long White assault upon the potlatch (see below) and the still unresolved question of native land title in British Columbia are the subjects of Forrest La Violette's *The Struggle for Survival* [134]. Attacked by certain historians as biased in favor of the natives and faulty in method, the study is nevertheless the best account in print of the circumstances surrounding the framing, passage, and enforcement of the now infamous Potlatch Law. This legislation, aimed against perhaps the most important ceremonial complex of the Northwest Coast peoples, outlawed the potlatch from 1883 to 1951. La Violette's discussion of the history of the dispossession of native lands throughout the province is at once brilliant and depressing.

An essential though rare source on the land rights

problem in British Columbia is the four-volume *Report of the Royal Commission on Indian Affairs for the Province of British Columbia* [28]. Because the native peoples of the Coast never signed formal treaties alienating their lands to the European intruders, the royal commission was established in 1912 to adjudicate native land claims and establish reserves. The *Report* contains the detailed claims of the groups that met with the commission, its determinations, and a full listing of the reserves established.

One consequence of systematic dispossession may be a partial retreat to the solace of the bottle. The effects of drinking are outlined in Edwin Lemert's "Alcohol and the Northwest Coast Indians" [135]. A far more positive response to European intrusion is examined in Philip Drucker's *The Native Brotherhoods* [71]. Drucker traces the history and assesses the effectiveness of the Native Brotherhoods of Alaska and British Columbia. Separately organized in Alaska (in 1912) and in British Columbia (in 1931), these intertribal organizations have united the native peoples for political and economic aims. They have focused upon racial pride and the struggle for land, fishing, and educational rights.

Other effects of European control upon native people in British Columbia are discussed in Robert Levine's *Native Languages and Culture* [136]. Containing interviews with individuals who recount the pressures put on them in boarding schools, this compilation features an excellent history by Robert Levine and Freda

Cooper on the suppression of native languages in British Columbia. It also contains Barbara Efrat's report on the Hesquiat project, a Nootka-sponsored program to preserve the language and wisdom of their old people. The status of the native peoples of British Columbia was exhaustively examined in Hawthorn, Belshaw, and Jamieson's *The Indians of British Columbia* [114]. Based on extensive studies carried out between 1954 and 1956, the study recommended that native people be accorded the full rights of citizens, be freed from forced changes of government or religion, and be encouraged to undertake self-administration. *The Indians of British Columbia* has effected numerous changes in the policies of the Department of Indian Affairs. The efficacy of these changes was in part the subject of the Fields and Stanbury report, *The Economic Impact of the Public Sector upon the Indians of British Columbia* [88], which suggested that substantial improvements had been made in the quality of education, social welfare, health and hospitalization, community development, and planning. It also pointed out many inequities in the provincial administration of justice. Fields and Stanbury recommended the continued development of local native self-government, specifically to direct economic growth, and they suggested that these local governments should have the ability to levy taxes without being liable to taxation themselves. Many of their recommendations have since been implemented by the provincial government.

The history of native and White relations in the states of Washington and Alaska have not been as well documented as those of British Columbia. Though natives in these states have been subjected to many of the same discriminatory sanctions suffered by the native peoples of British Columbia, the United States has not sponsored studies specifically concerned with the problems of the Coast groups. The United States confronted the land question in 1946 with the establishment of the Indian Land Claims Commission. This commission was empowered to hear native land claims and to award money compensation for lands found to have been improperly acquired. The reports, which served as the basis for claims suits by the western Washington groups, have recently been published in the American Indian Ethnohistory series [41, 42, 84, 100, 166, 197, 203, 204, 206, 208].

Uncommon Controversy, the report of a study group of the American Friends Service Committee [2], is the only publication concerning the still volatile fishing-rights controversy in Washington. The treaties signed there in 1854 and 1855 guaranteed continued native fishing rights "at all usual and accustomed grounds and stations" both on and off the reservations. The controversy began when the state of Washington restricted native fishing during the late 1940s in direct violation of the treaties. *Uncommon Controversy* is an uncommonly comprehensive survey of the treaties, United States Indian policy, the state fishing laws of Washington, the fish and their environment, and the current status of the struggle between the native fishers and the government. The recent (1975) Boldt decision allocating 50 percent of the fishing catch to the native groups has yet to be analyzed in print. The equally recent Alaska Native Land Claims settlement, allotting many thousand square miles and several million dollars to the various Alaskan aboriginal groups, has been the subject of Robert D. Arnold's comprehensive *Alaska Native Land Claims* [6].

The Art of the Northwest Coast

The native arts of the Northwest Coast today rank among the world's major art traditions. The artifacts were collected as curiosities by European explorers and travelers, and so by the 1880s well-financed expeditions were systematically combing the villages for objects. Significant portions of the early ehtnographies of Swan, Niblack, Boas, and others were devoted to the fascinating material culture of the Coast groups.

Among the first studies to focus primarily upon Northwest Coast art forms were "The Basketry of the Tlingit" [85] and "The Chilkat Blanket" [86]. Both were fully illustrated products of detailed museum and photodocumentary research, and they remain much consulted. One of the first major studies of non-Western art was Franz Boas's *Primitive Art* [24]. First published in 1927, this classic work analyzed the fundamental formal, representational, symbolic and stylistic traits of primitive art. Northwest Coast materials made up the bulk of Boas's sample.

A substantial portion of the increasing attention to Northwest Coast art was paid to the monumental crest, or totem, poles found throughout the northern reaches of the area. Charles Marius Barbeau published his voluminous *Totem Poles of the Gitksan* in 1929 [9]. A United States Forest Service project gathered and restored a large number of abandoned or decaying Tlingit poles in southeastern Alaska in 1938. Viola Garfield gathered the legends and histories of these poles and published them with many photographs in 1948 as *The Wolf and the Raven* [97]. Repeatedly reprinted, this volume has become the most widely available publication on crest poles. The finest study of crest poles, however, is Barbeau's two-volume compendium, *Totem Poles* [10]. Containing hundreds of photographs and the histories and legends of the poles, this important work has unfortunately been permitted to go out of print.

The first catalog of a significant portion of a major museum collection published in North America was Robert Davis's *Native Arts of the Pacific Northwest* [54]. Containing a brief analytic text and 194 plates of objects from the Rasmussen Collection of the Portland Art Museum, this volume set the tone and style for most of its many successors.

The first popularly available comprehensive survey of Northwest Coast art primarily in its sculptural forms was *Art of the Northwest Coast Indians,* by Robert

Inverarity [119]. It included an analysis of the art, brief notes on ethnology, and 279 plates gathered from an international assortment of museums. Far less well known, but of great scholarly importance, is Paul Wingert's study of art styles in traditional Coast Salish wood carving, *American Indian Sculpture* [220]. A very fine selection of artifacts appears in Frederick Dockstader's *Indian Art in America* [62]. Originally published in 1961 as part of the Carnegie Study of the Arts of the United States, it remains one of the most widely available studies of native American art. It was followed in 1965 by Bill Holm's masterly *Northwest Coast Indian Art* [117], which isolated principles governing certain aspects of the art of the Northern culture province and is still the finest scholarly examination of Northwest Coast art. Erna Gunther combined an updated presentation of the Rasmussen Collection materials with an excellent discussion of art's sacred and secular roles in her *Art in the Life of the Northwest Coast Indian* [106].

The mainly Kwakiutl holdings of the Museum of Anthropology of the University of British Columbia in Vancouver are the subject of *Art of the Kwakiutl Indians*, by Audrey Hawthorn [113]. Its 537 plates illustrate virtually every aspect of life in the Wakashan culture province. A large body of objects from neighboring areas is included for regional comparison. Hawthorn's descriptions of the roles of artifact types used in the winter ceremonials are especially valuable. Joan Jones's *Northwest Coast Basketry and Culture Change* [124] is an academic study of basketry types through the North Pacific Coast.

Many fine color photographs of Tlingit artifacts in the collections of two Russian Museums are published in *North American Indian Art* [176]. Several fine articles by Wilson Duff, Bill Holm, and the Haida artist, Bill Reid, accompany the many photographs contained in the landmark catalog, *Arts of the Raven* [79].

Norman Feder's *American Indian Art* [87] is the stylistic successor to Dockstader's earlier work. This extensive study contains a brief discussion of Coast art illustrated by fifty-five of the most aesthetically pleasing photographs of Northwest Coast artifacts found in any publication. The year 1971 also saw the publication of the elegiac *Out of Silence,* by William Reid, with photographs by Adelaide de Menil [165]. This gorgeous and widely available volume features numerous photographs of weathered crest poles and sculptures coupled with a particularly moving narrative by William Reid.

Bill Holm and William Reid recently collaborated in the very well illustrated but chatty *Form and Freedom* [118], in which the lack of focus or direction vitiates the effect of the dialogue. The decision to split many of its fine photographs across two pages further lessens the power of this promising volume.

Ulli Steltzer's *Indian Artists at Work* [185] is an excellent photo and field survey of the many artists and art forms currently active along the coast of British Columbia. Steltzer interviewed a large number of carvers, basket weavers, canoemakers, blanketmakers, and sweatermakers from the Nass River to the Cowichan reserve near Vancouver.

The Potlatch

Much creative effort went into display and distribution at the well-known potlatch ceremonies of the Northwest Coast. These are controversial in virtually all particulars, but most scholars support H. G. Barnett's definition of the potlatch as "a congregation of people, ceremoniously and often individually invited to witness a demonstration of family prerogative" [13]. The acceptance of gifts from the host of a potlatch represented a formal recognition of the status prerogatives claimed.

Few ceremonial institutions have received as much attention. Its spectacular oratory, elaborate form, and seeming disdain for enormous accumulations of wealth scandalized foreign observers. Missionaries succeeded in outlawing the ceremonies after correctly identifying them as the most important cultural event of the cultures they sought to obliterate; but potlatching has staged a healthy recovery throughout the Coast.

Potlatching has also inspired controversy among anthropologists, an admittedly contentious community to begin with. Boas presented the first highly detailed studies of the ceremonies as practiced by the Southern Kwakiutl of Fort Rupert on Vancouver Island during the 1880s and 1890s. Other scholars seized upon this information to support ideas that the potlatch was a primitive form of banking, a form of intergroup competition, or a strictly symbolic exercise. An absurd extreme was reached in a chapter of Ruth Benedict's influential *Patterns of Culture* [17]. Benedict used especially fulsome examples of Kwakiutl oratory as damning evidence of a megalomaniac paranoid "Dionysian" culture on the Northwest Coast. Offensively worded, even by the less sensitive standards of the 1930s, Benedict's study was nevertheless widely accepted and discussed. Even her opponents went to unfortunate lengths in characterizing the potlatch. Boas disagreed with Benedict's contention that any culture possessed a personality type, but he referred to the potlatch as "atrocious but amiable." This led Helen Codere to that emphasis in her article "The Amiable Side of Kwakiutl Life: The Potlatch and Play Potlatch" [37].

Codere presented another explanation for the potlatch in *Fighting with Property* [36], where she asserted that the violence and competition of potlatching replaced that of warfare within twenty years of the first intense European contacts in 1792. The reinterpretation of Kwakiutl potlatching as part of the "process of domesticating warfare into the service of all important rivalry for social prestige" served the cause of amiability without touching the central hypotheses of the potlatch as an expression of competitive rivalry and megalomania.

Barnett's belief that the potlatch validated rather than competitively redistributed status prerogatives was finally reconfirmed in Philip Drucker and Robert Heizer's *To Make My Name Good* [73]. This study further denied that potlatching redistributed periodically scarce resources.

Much interpretation of the potlatch assumes that the Northwest Coast was blessed with virtually unlimited resources and that such wealth produced leisure for the development of complex social institutions—a notion clearly invalidated by recent ethnographic data showing that "simple" hunting and gathering groups had more leisure time than the average American millionaire. Studies such as Woodcock's *Peoples of the Coast* [222] demonstrate that this information has not filtered down to all students of Northwest Coast culture.

Arguing that the Northwest Coast was not uniformly blessed with the abundance of nature, Wayne Suttles's influential "Affinal Ties, Subsistence, and Prestige among the Coast Salish" [192] suggested that the potlatch redistributed periodically scarce resources, most notably food, among disproportionately blessed groups in different habitats. This view was further publicized by A. P. Vayda's "A Re-examination of Northwest Coast Economic Systems" [211]. Vayda emphasized the potlatch as a vehicle to exchange food for wealth among Coast groups in need of either. These findings were reinforced by Stuart Piddocke's reexamination of the Southern Kwakiutl data in "The Potlatch System of the Southern Kwakiutl" [163]. Daniela Weinberg placed the redistribution hypothesis into systems theory terms in her "Models of Southern

Kwakiutl Social Organization" [216]. Suttles extended the range of this perspective to include the entire Northwest Coast in "Variation in Habitat and Culture on the Northwest Coast" [193] and "Coping with Abundance: Subsistence on the Northwest Coast" [194]. Most recently, John Adams has suggested that the redistribution of people was an effective way of redistributing resources. In his excellent study *The Gitksan Potlatch* [1] he demonstrated that people became the retainers of prosperous chiefs. A major mark of success was the ability to hold memorable potlatches. Those able to marshal goods and wealth from their home territories were thus able to attract retainers from less well endowed regions.

Reaction to the redistribution hypothesis set in quickly. Drucker and Heizer misrepresented it by angrily attacking the hypothesis as economic determinism and by alleging that its holders believed that Northwest Coast societies "lived constantly on the verge of starvation, warded off only by the food-for-wealth exchange." They presented evidence that starvation was unknown north of Coast Salish territory. Such statements were recently disputed by Leland Donald and Donald Mitchell in "Some Correlates of Local Rank among the Southern Kwakiutl" [63]. Utilizing modern salmon escapement figures to determine the extent of salmon runs in several rivers in Kwakiutl territory, these investigators discovered "important territorial and annual variations in the number of salmon available in the Southern Kwakiutl area." They further found direct correlation between the availability of salmon, group population, and local group rank.

The structural hypothesis of Abraham Rosman and Paula Rubel, set forth in their book *Feasting with Mine Enemy* [171] and their more accessible article "The Potlatch: A Structural Analysis" [172], stated that "the potlatch ceremony [was] an integral part of a distinct type of social system," the exchange society. This society was defined as a culture organized and ranked through a central exchange ceremony cementing reciprocal relationships both between and within groups. Rosman and Rubel further held that the type of exchange ceremony indicated the social structure of the group in question. They correlated differences in various Northwest Coast social structures with differences in their potlatch complexes.

Eugene Ruyle's "Slavery, Surplus and Stratification on the Northwest Coast" [173] presented the potlatch as a form of incipient church-state extortion that pumped energy into Northwest Coast society. Ruyle disputes what he terms the Suttles-Vayda hypothesis by stating that potlatching redistributed surplus rather than scarce resources. Sally Snyder has asserted that the Coast Salish regard food as ritually polluted. In her "Quest for the Sacred in Northern Puget Sound" [182] she noted that the potlatch involved the exchange of food for wealth and prestige, permitting the exchange of a despised but essential commodity for highly desirable wealth objects and prestige.

Irving Goldman, reviewing the original George

Hunt texts used by Franz Boas, has suggested that Boas mistranslated the Kwakiutl term for *giving* into *potlatch*. In *The Mouth of Heaven* [102], Goldman contends that potlatching did not exist as an exchange system in Kwakiutl society. The ceremony, he argues, was in actuality a nonmaterial major component of Kwakiutl cosmology primarily concerned with the great religious issues of life renewal. Bill Holm [118] has since demonstrated that Goldman, not Boas, mistranslated the Kwakiutl texts, thus invalidating much of Goldman's argument.

Many early Northwest Coast ethnographies recognized the presence of three classes—nobles, commoners, and slaves—in traditional Coast society. Philip Drucker, in "Rank, Wealth and Kinship in Northwest Coast Society" [64], countered this view with the assertion that rank rather than class characterized the stratification of Northwest Coast cultures. Thus, these societies consisted of a continual gradation of ranked status slots without class distinctions. Helen Codere corroborated Drucker's findings with an extensive interpretation of Southern Kwakiutl ethnohistoric data, "Kwakiutl Society: Rank without Class" [38]. And there the matter lay until revived in Vernon Kobrinsky's excellent, though obscurely published, "Dynamics of the Fort Rupert Class Struggle: Fighting with Property Vertically Revisited" [131]. Kobrinsky's reexamination of the Southern Kwakiutl data has clearly indicated that Drucker and Codere failed to recognize classes among the Kwakiutl more by choice than because of the force of the data. Kobrinsky has further found that the tremendous elaboration of potlatching during the historical contact period was part of the class struggle of traditional chiefs to maintain their hereditary control over the chiefly prerogatives in the face of stiff competition from nouveau riche commoners.

The Culture Provinces

The Northern Culture Province

The first major work on the aboriginal societies of the region was Albert Niblack's "The Coast Indians of Southern Alaska and Northern British Columbia" [153]. Ensign Niblack gathered a large body of information during his three-year tour of duty along the North Coast from 1885 to 1887. He supplemented it with information culled from published ethnographies and travel accounts from the area. Massively illustrated, his fine overview of North Coast culture has worn well and remains a much-consulted key source for the ethnology and history of the region.

Missionary William Collison's out-of-print memoir *In the Wake of the War Canoe* [43] has also stood the test of time. Those choosing to overlook the admittedly thick tributes to the triumph of faith over savagery and darkness will discover an impressively detailed and relatively dispassionate study. The history and ethnology of the Haida, Tsimshian, and now extinct

Athapaskan-speaking Coastal Tsetsaut (Collison's Zitz-Zaow tribe) during the last forty years of the nineteenth century receive excellent coverage.

Another out-of-print work is Theresa Mayer Durlach's overwhelming *The Relationship Systems of the Tlingit, Haida and Tsimshian* [82]. Based primarily upon the publications of Franz Boas, Edward Sapir, and John Swanton, it is a massive descriptive and comparative study of North Coast kinship systems.

Charles Marius Barbeau published the single extant study of North Coast shamanism in 1958 under the title *Medicine-Men on the North Pacific Coast* [12]. Well illustrated with ninety photographs of Haida argillite carvings and the many tools of Tsimshian and Haida practioners, this volume also includes three native accounts of healers gathered by William Beynon.

Less weighty is Edward Keithahn's *Monuments in Cedar* [127], which presents a competent overview of the "totempolar region" with a large selection of photographs. Among its findings are historical support for the recent independent invention of the crest pole on the Coast and evidence that the source for the metal used in the famous potlatch coppers was European rather than aboriginal, at least in coppers that have survived.

Tlingit

The first important ethnography of the Tlingit was Aurel Krause's *The Tlingit Indians* [133]. The result of a field trip to southeastern Alaska in 1880 and 1881,

Krause's study has remained the best general history and ethnology of the Tlingit-speaking groups. Erna Gunther's translation from the German is enhanced by references to more recent research, corrections, a bibliography, and an index. "The Basketry of the Tlingit" [85] and "The Chilkat Blanket" [86] contain a great deal of information on the gathering, processing, and fabrication of materials. Both studies also include valuable data on the sociological role of these objects in Tlingit life.

The ethnologist John Swanton visited the Tlingit of Wrangell and Sitka during the first four months in 1904. Recognizing the work of Krause and Emmons, Swanton concentrated upon gathering linguistic and ethnological data from his informants. He published them as "Social Condition, Beliefs, and Linguistic Relationship of the Tlingit Indians" [202]. Swanton's excellent study was followed by a considerably less valuable book by Livingston Jones entitled *A Study of the Thlingets of Alaska* [125]. First published in 1914 and recently reprinted, this book has also received the recommendation of Murdock and O'Leary as a key work on the Tlingit. Though it contains good descriptions of Tlingit economy and cultural status on the eve of World War I, it is riddled with ethnocentric observations. Jones's beliefs that the Tlingit were degenerate Japanese, that their language was "stunted and dwarfed," having little in it "to merit perpetuation," and that Tlingit women were primarily gossips and troublemakers require no further comment.

Another book that tells more about the prejudices

of its author than about the Tlingit people is O. M. Salisbury's *The Customs and Legends of the Thlinget Indians of Alaska* [174]. Based upon the author's experiences while a government functionary and entrepreneur at the village of Klawock during the 1920s, it has little to recommend it.

Kalervo Oberg's *The Social Economy of the Tlingit Indians* [155] is the best study of the relationship between environment and Tlingit social organization. Researched at the village of Klukwan in 1931 and 1932, this publication of Oberg's doctoral dissertation was a long-awaited and happily received addition to Tlingit ethnography. Oberg's chapter on the annual cycle of production is particularly valuable. The volume includes a foreward by Wilson Duff and comments by Tlingit lawyer and grand president emeritus of the Alaska Native Brotherhood, William L. Paul, Sr.

The results of Ronald Olson's field trips throughout Tlingit territory during the summers of 1933, 1934, 1949, and 1954 were published in 1967 as "Social Structure and Social Life of the Tlingit in Alaska" [160]. Noting that Tlingit culture was remarkable uniform throughout its range from Yakutat Bay south to the British Columbia border, Olson generally corroborated Swanton's findings concerning Tlingit political, social, and religious life. Frances Paul's *The Spruce Root Basketry of the Tlingit* [161] is both a how-to guide to the subject and a remarkably complete and thoroughly illustrated survey of the many weaves and design types of Tlingit spruce-root basketry, written by a Tlingit craftswoman.

The cooperative fieldwork of Catharine McClellan and Frederica De Laguna conducted during the late 1940s and early 1950s has paid particularly handsome dividends. McClellan describes how Tlingit ceremonialism strengthened and reaffirmed their basic social groupings in her article, "The Interrelationships of Social Structure with Northern Tlingit Ceremonialism" [139]. De Laguna isolates and analyzes the major divisions of Tlingit social structure and the factors affecting community stability and instability in "Some Dynamic Forces in Tlingit Society" [55]. Her further study, "Tlingit Ideas about the Individual" [56], disclosed that such ideas were not limited to a single distinct self but were compounded and linked with ancestors, descendants, contemporaries, supernatural beings, and portions of the inanimate world. (The average Tlingit person was rarely lonely.)

De Laguna's three-volume magnum opus *Under Mount Saint Elias* [58] is the most nearly definitive ethnography of a Northwest Coast group. Virtually every known aspect of Yakutat geography, environment, history (both native and nonnative), economy, society, religion, and cosmology comes under intense scrutiny. Impeccably documented and admirable in scope, the third volume also contains 218 plates, 138 transcriptions of Yakutat songs, and a thorough index.

An impressive review of general Tlingit ethnohistory has been written by the Soviet ethnologist Julia Averkieva. Entitled "The Tlingit Indians" [8], it draws upon a number of nineteenth-century Russian sources to fill out incompletely known aspects of Tlingit clan organization, slavery, social stratification, and potlatching. More recently, Laura Klein has presented a rare view of women's roles in her doctoral dissertation, "Tlingit Women and Town Politics" [130].

Haida

The first and best full-dress ethnography of traditional Haida sociocultural life on the Queen Charlotte Islands was John Swanton's *Contributions to the Ethnology of the Haida* [201]. Swanton collected his data primarily from two Skidegate informants between September 1900 and August 1901. Not concerned with Haida material culture, Swanton's exhaustive documentation of a wide variety of family crests, names, songs, clans, and towns remains an essential source of Haida ethnography.

Drawing largely upon Swanton to flesh out the accounts of his unidentified informants, Edward Curtis published a brief and poorly organized schematic view of traditional Haida culture as part of volume 11 of his twenty-volume work *The North American Indians* [48]. Curtis's sketch of the Haida is the poorest in his three volumes devoted to Northwest Coast culture.

George Murdock wrote a highly detailed portrait of Haida social organization in his "Kinship and Social Behavior among the Haida" [150]. Using data gathered during a summer field trip in 1932, Murdock described the various kinship systems of the Skidegate, Masset, and Hydaburg, or Alaskan, Haida. He followed this study with an excellent account of potlatching and social class entitled "Rank and Potlatch among the Haida" [151]. This article came under attack by Drucker in his 1939 attempt to disprove the existence of social classes along the Coast.

A Popular digest of these sources appeared in *Haida*, by A. F. Flucke and A. E. Pickford [90]. This widely available survey volume was followed by Charles Marius Barbeau's *Haida Carvers in Argillite* [11]. Impressively illustrated with 227 photographs of carvers and of the black slate carvings produced especially for foreign sale, this volume contains the biographies of more than fifty Haida sculptors.

Another fine study is the detailed description by Wilson Duff and Michael Kew of Haida settlements on one of the southernmost islands of the Queen Charlotte chain. Published in the hard-to-obtain *Annual Report* of the British Columbia Provincial Museum, "Anthony Island, a Home of the Haidas" [80] focuses upon the famous village of Ninstints, abandoned sometime during the late 1880s. A good selection of ethnohistorical accounts of events associated with the village animates the archaeological and ethnographic data presented in this report of the 1957 expedition to survey and salvage Haida monuments on the island.

Anthony Carter's *This Is Haida* [33] is a stunning tour guide of the modern Queen Charlotte Islands. Many radiant color photographs illuminate views of Haida life, decaying vestiges of Haida sculpture reclaimed by the rain forest, and the magnificent scenery of the archipelago.

Margaret Blackman's "Totems to Tombstones" [19] and "The Northern and Kaigani Haida" [18] are excellent ethnohistorical analyses of Haida culture change over the past hundred years. A less effective comparative study of the effects of contact upon the Masset and Skidegate groups of the Queen Charlotte Islands during the same period is presented in J. H. Van den Brink's *The Haida Indians* [210].

The Totem Poles of Skedans, by John and Carolyn Smyly [181], is an unusual account of the construction of a miniature replica of the Haida village of Skedans for the British Columbia Provincial Museum in Victoria. Relying almost entirely upon George Dawson's photographs of the site, the Smylys describe fifty-six crest poles and depict them in sketches and photographs.

Tsimshian

The Tsimshian of the northernmost portion of coastal British Columbia consist of three linguistic and sociocultural divisions—the Nishga of the Nass River valley, the Coast Tsimshian to the north and south of the mouth of the Skeena River, and the Gitksan of the upper Skeena River valley. A popular introduction to all of these groups may be found in A. F. Flucke and A. E. Pickford's *Tsimshian* [95]. A more scholarly review of general Tsimshian studies is Wilson Duff's "Contri-

butions of Marius Barbeau to West Coast Ethnology"
[75]. Duff discusses Barbeau's field research among the
Tsimshian, conducted with William Beynon between
1914 and 1947, and reviews Barbeau's hypotheses of
the Asiatic origins of shamanism and ceremonialism
and the postcontact origin of crest poles along the
Coast. Duff's conclusion that Barbeau was wrong on
both counts has been corroborated by recent archaeological findings indicating aboriginal development of classic Northwest Coast culture. A biography
of Barbeau's assistant, and a guide to and assessment of
Barbeau's data (the bulk of which remains in manuscript form) may be found in Marjorie Halpin's excellent article "William Beynon, Tsimshian, 1888–1958"
[111].

Little is known about the Nishga. Collison [43] describes their subsistence and missionization. Edward
Sapir's "A Sketch of the Social Organization of the
Nass River Indians" [175] briefly presents the results of
a somewhat hurried meeting with four Nishga men
visiting Ottawa during 1915 and lists the four Nishga
groups with their kinship and crest systems, house and
personal names, and social classes.

The Coast Tsimshian have been the subjects of extensive investigations. The first volumes devoted to
their culture and history were *The Story of Metlakahtla*
by Henry Wellcome [217] and *The Apostle of Alaska* by
John Arctander [4]. Both long out of print, they contain information gathered by the famous missionary
William Duncan on Tsimshian culture and the Met-

lakatla mission. While blatantly biased in favor of the controversial Duncan, both volumes are excellent surveys of the mission situated successively in British Columbia (Wellcome) and New Metlakatla, Annette Island, Alaska (Arctander). A more modern account devoted to the first British Columbia mission through 1887 may be found in Jean Usher's *William Duncan of Metlakatla* [209].

The finest single Tsimshian ethnography is Franz Boas's *Tsimshian Mythology* [22]. Based upon data drawn from Henry Tate of Port Simpson between 1902 and 1914, this volume has a rather full reconstruction of traditional Coast Tsimshian culture synthesized from Tate's and Boas's cooperative analyses of Tsimshian oral literature.

Willaim Beynon served as Viola Garfield's major informant and interpreter during her research for *Tsimshian Clan and Society* at Port Simpson during the summers of 1932, 1935, and 1937 [96]. This detailed but hard-to-get description of the traditional Coast Tsimshian social order was later rewritten as *The Tsimshian: Their Arts and Music* [98], containing articles by Paul Wingert and Charles Marius Barbeau. It was rereleased in 1966, without Barbeau's article, under the title *The Tsimshian Indians and Their Arts* [99]. This latest incarnation of Garfield's work continues as the best-known and most accessible volume on Tsimshian culture.

Majorie Halpin's recent dissertation, "The Tsimshian Crest System" [110], is a masterly structural analysis of Coast Tsimshian social organization as seen through the crest masks and texts collected by William Beynon and Henry Tate. A historical survey of changes in Coast Tsimshian potlatching may be found in Robert Grumet's "Changes in Coast Tsimshian Redistributive Activities in the Fort Simpson Region of British Columbia, 1788–1862" [103].

Little has been published on the Southern Coast Tsimshian of Kitkatla, Hartley Bay, and China Hat. Even less has appeared on the Canyon, or Kitselas, Tsimshian of the lower Skeena River valley.

The first major study of the Gitksan was Charles Marius Barbeau's *Totem Poles of the Gitksan* [9]. First published in 1929, it describes owners, origins, functions, and carvers of the poles in four Gitksan villages, supplemented by discussions of Gitksan social organization and a large selection of plates showing the poles themselves.

The highly conservative Kitwancool requested and received the assistance of British Columbia Provincial Museum ethnologists in 1958 to preserve their crest poles and history. Wilson Duff edited the project's excellent *Histories, Territories, and Laws of the Kitwancool* [78].

A further symptom of Gitksan resurgence has been the establishment of the Ksan museum and craft program in Hazelton, British Columbia. Ksan houses the only school teaching Northwest Coast art, and their efforts have materially assisted in the preservation of many aspects of traditional Gitksan culture. These

developments are documented in the stunning catalog
'*KSAN: Breath of Our Grandfathers*, edited by George
MacDonald [141].
Sumptuous color vistas of the spectacular Gitksan
country and photos of modern Gitksan life appear in
Anthony Carter's *Abundant Rivers* [34]. John Adams's
study *The Gitksan Potlatch* [1], researched between 1965
and 1967, contains an excellent analysis of the relationship between people, resources, crests, and potlatching.
The recently published *Visitors Who Never Left*, translated by Kenneth B. Harris from stories taped by his
uncle, Arthur McDames, in 1948 [112], presents eight
traditional Gitksan historical accounts of their home-
land, Damelahamid, situated along the wide valley of
the upper Skeena River.

Northern Kwakiutl

The immediate neighbors of the southern Coast
Tsimshian, the Kwakiutl-speaking Xaihais, Heiltsuk,
and Haisla, of the Milbanke Sound and Kitimat drain-
age region, share a lack of scholarly recognition. They
have been regarded as infertile ground for ethnographic inquiry because of the disappearance of the
traditional culture and the intransigence of the communities, and no major ethnographic or ethnohistorical study has been attempted among these groups.
Scattered references to Northern Kwakiutl groups,
coupled with a brief listing of their sociopolitical divi-

sions, appear in Edward Curtis's *The Kwakiutl* [50]. Ivan Lopatin's fieldwork among the Haisla during the summer of 1930 appeared in 1945 as *Social Life and Religion of the Indians in Kitimat, British Columbia* [138]. Competently describing the objects of his study, Lopatin anticipated Ruth Benedict in characterizing Haisla interest in wealth and prestige as a "megalomaniac philosophy" that made "the behavior of the Kitimat . . . very peculiar." Such statements may explain why the Northern Kwakiutl have been generally unresponsive to fieldwork.

Ronald Olson conducted fieldwork at Kitimat and Rivers Inlet in 1935 and at Bella Bella during 1935 and 1949. Studies made at the first locations were published in 1955 under the title "Notes on the Bella Bella Kwakiutl" [159]. This work contained listings of village-tribes, kinship groups and terminologies, names, titles, and other objects of sociocultural interest. The latter research had earlier produced Olson's "The Social Organization of the Haisla" [157].

Philip Drucker described the secret society dances of the Heiltsuk, Xaihais, and Haisla (Xaisla) in "Kwakiutl Dancing Societies" [65]. Having collected his data during the winter of 1936–37, Drucker delineated two or three distinct ceremonial systems in contrast to the single winter ceremony of the Southern Kwakiutl reported by Franz Boas (see below). Drucker published further Northern Kwakiutl data in "Culture Element Distribution Number 26: Northwest Coast" [67]. A brief color-photo essay on modern fishing at Kynoc has been included in Anthony Carter's *Somewhere Between* [32].

The Wakashan Culture Province

Southern Kwakiutl

The Southern Kwakiutl inhabit the mountainous coasts of northeastern Vancouver Island and the adjacent mainland. They number some twenty politically and territorially distinct divisions, each organized into several ambilineal kinship groups known as *numaym* (pl. *numayma*). The magnificient potlatches and dramatic winter ceremonials that link the Kwakiutl's sacred and secular worlds have made them the best-studied people of the Coast.

Examples of Kwakiutl material culture collected by Johan Adrian Jacobsen and conversations with ethnologists Aurel and Arthur Krause stimulated the interest of the young German geographer Franz Boas. Beginning his researches in 1886, Boas produced a vast scholarly output spanning the following forty-five years that brought worldwide attention to the Southern Kwakiutl. Much of it was gathered with the assistance of the brilliant Kwakiutl informant George Hunt, and it has supported the burden of numerous ethnological investigations by other scholars. Boas's first major publication on Kwakiutl ethnography was "The Social Organization and Secret Societies of the Kwakiutl Indians" [20]. First published in 1897, this is a copiously illustrated classic in ethnographic reportage. Boas's "The Kwakiutl of Vancouver Island" [21], based upon observations made during the Jesup North Pacific Expedition, remains the most complete statement on Southern Kwakiutl material culture. Cultural lacunae were filled in *Contributions to the Ethnology of the Kwakiutl* [23]. Boas died before he was able to publish his comprehensive one-volume *Kwakiutl Ethnography* [25]. Edited by Helen Codere, Boas's incomplete manuscript has been filled out with several key selections from his major works, a full bibliography of his publications, and an index. Containing the best of Boas's Kwakiutl data, his chapters on social organization, shamanism, and the winter ceremonial represent his final and fullest statements on the subjects.

Massive descriptions of the winter ceremonial and a wide selection of excellent photographs make Edward Curtis's *The Kwakiutl* [50] an enduring classic of Southern Kwakiutl ethnography. It also has adequate discussions of traditional subsistence and material culture.

Clellan S. Ford edited the autobiography of the Kwakiutl chief Charley Nowell, *Smoke from Their Fires,* in 1941 [154]. This fine document traces Nowell's life in great detail, describing his childhood, education, and rise in the Fort Rupert Kwakiutl ritual hierarchy.

Helen Codere added a much-needed historical dimension to Kwakiutl ethnography in her previously mentioned *Fighting with Property* [36] and her more comprehensive "Kwakiutl" [39]. The latter contains a highly detailed review of Kwakiutl contact history, divided into the "Pre-Potlatch" (1770–1849), "Potlatch" (1849–1921), and "Post-Potlatch" (1921–55) periods. Impressed by the successful adaptation of the Kwakiutl to White intrusion, she credits the continuance of Kwakiutl survival to fundamental similarities in both cultures.

Ronald Olson presents an extensive account of Kwakiutl life in "Social Life of the Owikeno Kwakiutl" [158]. A fine general popular introduction to the Kwakiutl may be found in A. F. Flucke and A. E. Pickford's *Kwakiutl* [93]. Ronald Rohner's *The People of Gilford* [168] and its more popular and available version, *The Kwakiutl*, written with Evelyn Rohner [170], are the first studies of a contemporary Southern Kwakiutl community. Based upon the Rohner's field experiences from September 1962 to August 1963, with another visit during the summer of 1964, these books focus upon the social life of Gilford Island. However, their emphasis upon the negative features of "conflict as a distinctive feature of normal interaction" and the problem of intoxication have not sat well with either the community or other scholars.

The finest autobiography of a modern Southern Kwakiutl chief is *Guests Never Leave Hungry,* the life of Chief James Sewid [183]. Edited by James Spradley and containing an exceptional analysis of bicultural adaptation, this is the best account of the modern Southern Kwakiutl.

Harry Wolcott wrote a highly detailed description of schooling at the pseudonymous Blackfish Village, *A Kwakiutl Village and School* [221], and Peter Macnair recently published two photographic essays of modern winter dancing and potlatching at Alert Bay [145].

Bella Coola

The single major scholarly study of the Coast Salish–speaking Bella Coola is T. F. McIlwraith's two-volume *The Bella Coola Indians* [143]. Based upon data collected from a single village in March through August 1922 and between September 1923 and February 1924, the work reconstructs traditional Bella Coola society. It has never been reprinted, but McIlwraith's findings are popularly available in his *Bella Coola* volume of the British Columbia Heritage series [144].

Margaret Stott presents a survey in *Bella Coola Ceremony and Art* [189]. Stott discusses the relationship between aspects of material culture and cosmology, one of the areas not covered in McIlwraith's monograph. Harlan Ingersoll Smith, who accompanied McIlwraith on the 1922 field trip, published part of his findings in "Materia Medica of the Bella Coola and Neighbouring Tribes of British Columbia" [178]. Surprisingly little else of substance on the Bella Coola has appeared in print, and the major study on the group has been unavailable for many years.

Nootka

The Nootka of the west coast of Vancouver Island and Cape Flattery were among the first Northwest Coast groups to experience intense European contact during the latter part of the eighteenth century. The first considerable account of the Nootka was written by Captain James Cook during his one-month stay at Friendly Cove on his third voyage in 1778. His detailed description of their social life and subsistence activities, coupled with a vocabulary of Nootka words, appears in his often-reprinted *The Journals of Captain James Cook on His Voyages of Discovery* [45].

Large numbers of American and Spanish ships followed Cook to Nootka Sound during the late 1770s. A very fine Spanish description of the Nootka made during the 1792 Bodega y Quadra expeditions has been published in *Noticias de Nutka* [149]. It is accompanied by translator and editor Iris Higbie Wilson's discussion of Spanish penetration of the coast and the English response, which almost led to a war between the two powers.

The trading vessel *Boston* was attacked and burned at Nootka Sound on 22 March 1803. One of the two survivors, John Jewitt, became a slave of the Nootka chief Macquinna. His captivity narrative, *The Adventures and Sufferings of John R. Jewitt* [122], is a highly detailed account of Nootkan culture based on his stay among the Nootka from 1803 to 1805. This frequently republished volume has remained the best source on aboriginal Nootkan culture, a rare inside view of a Northwest Coast society at the dawn of European intrusion. The first general ethnographic survey of the Nootkan groups of the west coast of Vancouver Island was Gilbert Sproat's remarkable *Scenes and Studies of Savage Life* [184]. Based upon his experiences among what he termed the "Aht" people between 1860 and 1868, Sproat's volume is a surprisingly complete account of Nootkan culture and a pragmatic guide to harmonious relations with one's Nootkan neighbors. Still out of print, this sadly neglected volume is representative of the best of pre-Boasian ethnography on the Northwest Coast.

Edward Curtis published a somewhat schematic overview of Nootka culture in British Columbia and Washington in *The Nootka, The Haida* [51], with emphasis on the spectacular nature of Nootkan whaling.

The linguist Edward Sapir worked among the Nootka sporadically from 1910 until 1933. Publishing extensively on Nootkan linguistics and myth, he produced little of completely ethnographic interest during his life. It was left to his students and colleagues to edit and publish his many manuscripts and to interpret his data ethnologically. Morris Swadesh produced the much-consulted "Motivations in Nootka Warfare" in 1948, basing his analysis upon Sapir's collection of nine war narratives [198]. Helen Roberts and Morris Swadesh later published a detailed analysis of ninety-nine songs collected by Sapir in their *Songs of the Nootka Indians of Western Vancouver Island* [167].

Vincent Koppert worked among the Clayoquot of

the Opitsit reserve during the summers of 1923 and 1929. Primarily interested in their material culture, he published his findings in *Contributions to Clayoquot Ethnology* [132]. This volume was followed by Philip Drucker's *The Northern and Central Nootkan Tribes* [68]. This magnificently detailed survey of Nootkan culture and society was compiled from field research conducted between 1935 and 1937.

An adequate popular introduction to the Nootka of British Columbia may be found in A. F. Flucke and A. E. Pickford's *Nootka* [94]. A very fine fictionalized story of a Nootkan potlatch is George Clutesi's *Potlatch* [35]. Eugene Arima's well-illustrated and impeccably documented monograph *A Report on a West Coast Whaling Canoe Reconstructed at Port Renfrew, B.C.* [5] is the best study of Northwest Coast dugout canoe technology. Having observed the construction of a west coast or "Nootka" canoe by three traditional canoe-builders, Arima supplements his step-by-step description with an ethnohistorical and ethnological analysis.

The Nootkan-speaking Makah of Cape Flattery have attracted considerable individual attention, primarily because they are the only Nootkan group resident in the United States and are thus more readily accessible to American scholars than their remote Northern and Central relatives. The first major study of the Makah was James Swan's *The Indians of Cape Flattery* [200]. The 1960 edition is a reprint of the original 1869 edition, without the preface, table of contents, and index. It remains, however, the best account of traditional Makah life.

T. T. Waterman's *The Whaling Equipment of the Makah Indians* is a fine study of Makah whaling based upon data provided by a traditional Makah whaler [212]. Well illustrated, with many technical details, it included an account of a whale hunt and its aftermath.

Ethnomusicologist Frances Densmore collected 199 songs at Neah Bay during the summers of 1923 and 1926, including fifty-three Clayoquot and ten Quileute melodies, which she published in 1939 as *Nootka and Quileute Music* [60]. The book is wonderfully detailed, with biographies of her informants, extensive ethnographic information, and a fine ethnobotany.

The Makah response to American intrusion is the subject of Elizabeth Colson's *The Makah Indians* [44]. In perhaps the best acculturation study of a Northwest Coast people, Colson concludes that by 1953 the Makah had weathered eighty years of intensive White contact. Though they have become assimilated into American society to a great extent, she states that they are, and will remain, a distinct group. She credits their persistence to their privileged federal status as reservation Indians.

The Makah successfully litigated for compensation for their lands by the Indian Land Claims Commission. Herbert Taylor established the archaeological and ethnographic heritage of the Makah in his report, "Anthropological Investigation of the Makah Indians" [204]. A rather stunted "History of the Neah Bay Agency," by Alix Gillis [100], features demographic data culled from reports of Indian agents to the commissioner of Indian affairs from 1857 to 1912 and from 1928 to 1932.

The Coast Salish–Chemakum Culture Province

The Coast Salish- and Chemakum-speaking peoples inhabit the islands, inlets, beaches, and rivers of the Gulf of Georgia in British Columbia, the international border zone of the Strait of Juan de Fuca, and Puget Sound and the Olympic Peninsula of Washington State. The native peoples fished, gathered, and hunted in a particularly favored region, dwelling in villages containing numbers of long plank houses, each sheltering a patrilineal descent group. Celebrants of the Guardian Spirit ceremonies, long supernatural shamanistic spirit canoe voyages, and extravagant potlatch feasts, the Coast Salish and Chemakum have been closely observed by their Canadian and American neighbors for more than 150 years. Living cheek by jowl with the Vancouver and Seattle metropolitan areas, the native peoples of the region have alternately suffered and benefited from such proximity.

The first general description of the Coast Salish was made by the Canadian artist Paul Kane during his 1847 tour through Puget Sound and southeastern Vancouver Island. Kane's observations and paintings of the people, their villages, and their society [126] constitute a unique record of the early historical contact period. More than sixty years passed before another artist came to paint and document the Coast Salish and Chemakum. Edward Curtis's elegantly photographed and informative (if rambling) survey *The Salishan Tribes of the Coast* [49] describes traditional life from the Cowlitz above the Columbia River north to the Halkomelen-speaking Cowichan of southwestern British Columbia. A particularly valuable feature of this volume is Curtis's brief discussion of Chemakum culture and history.

The culture province came under organized scholarly scrutiny during the 1935–48 Columbia University "Coast Salish Project." Its results were published in Marian Smith's *Indians of the Urban Northwest* [180], with fourteen articles covering a wide range of Coast Salish subjects. Especially important are Trinita Rivera's "Diet of a Food Gathering People," Erna Gunther's "The Shaker Church," and June Collins's biography of the Skagit shaman John Fornsby. Though dated and in need of revision, *Indians of the Urban Northwest* remains the best modern survey of the Coast Salish and Chemakum in print.

Wendy Stuart's *Gambling Music of the Coast Salish Indians* is an introduction to the music and customs associated with the slahal game [190]. Wayne Suttles's "On the Cultural Trail of the Sasquatch" [195] reviews the Coast Salish beliefs connected with the creature popularly known as "Bigfoot."

Coast Salish of British Columbia

The Coast Salish of British Columbia are represented by three major groups, the northernly Comox, the Cowichan of the greater Vancouver area and the adjacent area of Vancouver Island, and the Klallam of the confluence of the Gulf of Georgia, Strait of Juan de Fuca, and Puget Sound. The first major survey of these groups was H. G. Barnett's densely detailed and inaccessible "Culture Element Distribution Number 9: Gulf of Georgia Salish" [14]. Barnett's data, which include the Bella Coola, were gathered from thirteen communities during 1934 and 1936. Much of this information was synthesized, rewritten, and made more accessible through Barnett's *The Coast Salish of British Columbia* [15], which presented a comprehensive overview of the Georgia Strait Salish.

A serviceable introduction to the British Columbia Coast Salish can be found in A. F. Flucke and A. E. Pickford's *Coast Salish* [91]. Photographic and descriptive excursions through the Gulf of Georgia region appear in Anthony Carter's *Somewhere Between* [32] and *Abundant Rivers* [34]. These expensively produced accounts of modern Coast Salish life are difficult to locate and not particularly scholarly. But they are competently written, highly sympathetic to their subject, and wonderfully illustrated with color photographs.

The first major study of Cowichan culture was the Reverend Thomas Crosby's *Among the An-Ko-Me-Nums*

[47]. A rambling and often offensively worded account of his observations among the Cowichan between 1862 and 1907, this book lists potlatching, ice bathing, and head flattening among the many evils of aboriginal society. Self-serving and pompous, it clearly illuminates the intolerance that led to the systematic persecution of adherents to the old ways during the late nineteenth and early twentieth centuries.

Diamond Jenness's presentation of Simon Pierre's *The Faith of a Coast Salish Indian* [121] is a view of Coast Salish cosmology. Jenness collected Pierre's ontological concepts while visiting the Katzie reserve in 1936. Bound with this account is Wayne Suttles's *Katzie Ethnographic Notes* [196]. Also based upon information furnished by Simon Pierre, this volume describes Katzie identity, neighboring groups, habitat, subsistence, and kinship, including Pierre's genealogy.

Wilson Duff prepared the first modern ethnography of a Cowichan group in 1952. *The Upper Stalo Indians of the Fraser Valley, British Columbia* [74] contains a wide range of sociocultural and ethnohistorical data gathered from six informants during the summers of 1949 and 1950. Duff also surveys ethnohistorical documentation and ethnographic reportage.

Claudia Lewis's *Indian Families of the Northwest Coast* [137] is a more modestly focused study of culture change among the fictitiously named Camas band of Vancouver Island. Based on data gathered between 1954 and 1967, Lewis's thorough overview of modern Coast Salish life emphasizes an understanding of underlying motives and value systems in order to explain native culture change. Some of her recommendations appear later in the Fields and Stanbury report [88].

Wolfgang Jilek's superb *Salish Indian Mental Health and Culture Change* [123] is the most thorough study of the modern Guardian Spirit dance. Marvelously erudite and methodical, Jilek convincingly delineates the adaptive advantages of this much-maligned and formerly outlawed socioreligious complex.

Coast Salish and Chemakum of Western Washington State

The Coast Salish of western Washington include the Klallam, Twana, Snuqualmi, and Quinault. The Chemakum language isolate includes the now-extinct Chemakum proper and the Quileute and Hoh of the Olympic Peninsula. The best single survey of all of these groups continues to be Ruth Underhill's widely available and well-illustrated *Indians of the Pacific Northwest* [207].

The early work of T. T. Waterman at the turn of this century has also worn well. His *Types of Canoes on Puget Sound* [214], written in collaboration with G. Coffin, and *Indian Homes of Puget Sound,* with Ruth Griener [215], describe Twana, Klallam, and Snuqualmi house and canoe types. Attention to modes of production and societal roles enhances the continuing ethnological value of these monographs. Waterman's significant research on the poorly known material culture of the Twana and Snuqualmi was published in 1973 as *Notes on the Ethnology of the Indians of Puget Sound* [213]. Well documented, it illustrates many artifact types.

H. G. Barnett's *Indian Shakers* [16] traces the formative years of the Shaker religion between the "first death" of its founder John Slocum in 1882 and his second and final demise sometime before 1900. The church was founded after Slocum's first death, or vision experience; the name comes from the shaking that followed the entrance of a spirit into an adherent. The Shakers' many Christian attributes deflected missionary persecution of this otherwise clearly indentifiable successor of the traditional Guardian Spirit complex.

Erna Gunther's recently reprinted *Ethnobotany of Western Washington* continues as the most readily available source on Coast Salish, Quileute, and Makah food, medicine, and material plants [108]. Well documented, but indifferently illustrated, this classic study has been eclipsed by Turner's more recent guidebook [205]. A comprehensive early survey of Puget Sound native culture and "progress" is Myron Eells's "The Twana, Chemakum, and Klallum Indians of Washington Territory" [83].

Erna Gunther's *Klallam Ethnography* [104] was the first modern ethnological description. Using research conducted in 1924 and 1925, Gunther extensively reviewed past ethnographic and ethnohistorical documentation. Bernhard Stern's *The Lummi Indians of Northwest Washington* was the first analysis of this Klallam-speaking group [186]. First published in 1934 and based upon fieldwork performed in 1928 and 1929, Stern's brief and disappointingly schematic presentation concentrated upon contemporary Lummi spirit dancing and a reconstruction of traditional sociocultural forms. A number of Stern's epistemological shortcomings were recognized and partly eased in Wayne Suttles's work "Economic Life of the Coast Salish of Haro and Rosario Straits" [197]. Researched between 1946 and 1950, this remains the best subsistence analysis of the Coast. Also see Suttles [191].

Carroll Riley utilized a substantial portion of Lummi data in his delineation of the history and geographical background of the Coast Salish. His "Investigations and Analysis of the Puget Sound Indians" compiled for the Indian Land Claims Commission [166], established that the Lummi and other Puget Sound groups were recognizable sociopolitical entities with the village as the primary social unit.

Hermann Haeberlin conducted fieldwork among the Snohomish and Snuqualmi proper at the Tulalip Reservation in 1916 and 1917 and recorded many native terms for sociocultural phenomena. Haeberlin died before he could see the work into print, and it was left to the young Erna Gunther to publish it in German in 1924. Appearing in English in 1930 as *Indians of Puget Sound* [109], it has remained a perennial favorite.

Marian Smith's monograph *The Puyallup-Nisqually* [179] is the product of field research undertaken from 1935 to 1936. Exhaustively detailed and well documented, this reconstruction of traditional Puyallup-

Nisqually culture is the best ethnography of a Snuqualmi group.

June Collins has conducted field research among the Skagit at various times since 1942. Her first publication, "A Study of Religious Change among the Skagit Indians of Washington" [42], assessed the reasons why the Shaker church triumphed over the blandishments of Catholic missionaries in the Skagit villages. Collins concluded that Catholicism lost out because it failed to prevent killing and drinking and did not value certain Skagit ethical precepts that Shakerism respected. Her second publication, "Influence of White Contact on the Indians of Northern Puget Sound" [41], found that aboriginal rank and class hierarchies became more elaborated and more clearly defined as the pace of European intrusion increased.

June Collins finally published her definitive study of Upper Skagit culture and history in 1974. Entitled *Valley of the Spirits* [40] this ethnographic reconstruction describes their socio-cultural life, their ethnohistory, and Collin's methodology.

Colin Tweddell's "Historical and Ethnological Study of the Snohomish Indian People" [206] demonstrated that this group was both an aboriginal and a historical sociopolitical entity. Astutely utilizing historical, ethnographic, and informant-furnished data, this ethnohistorical review further found that the Stillaguamish, often considered a part of the Snohomish, were in fact a distinct group.

"Anthropological Investigations of the Medicine

Creek Tribes," by Herbert Taylor [203], faced the problem of determining the identities of the many groups who signed the 26 December 1854 Treaty of Medicine Creek and tracing their descendants. Through a combination of archaeological, ethnohistorical, ethnological, and ethnographic research strategies, Taylor established that the Squaxon, Puyallup, Nisqually, and Steilacoom groups who signed the treaty device had held aboriginal title to the lands so alienated. He found that the modern Steilacoom are not descendants of the historical participants of the Medicine Creek treaty but are primarily of Klallam and Cowlitz extraction.

An ethnography solely devoted to the Twana of the Hood Canal and the western shores of Puget Sound is William Elmendorf's massive *The Structure of Twana Culture* [84]. Based upon informant data furnished between 1939 and 1956, this extensive ethnographic reconstruction of traditional Skokomish-Twana culture ranks as one the premier studies of the region.

The first brief descriptions of the Quinault of the Pacific shore of the Olympic Peninsula were written by the pioneer James Swan. His most accessible published observations of this group and its neighbors can be found in his recently republished *The Northwest Coast* [199]. First published in 1857, this volume contains a wealth of anecdotal and ethnographic data on the peoples of the western slopes of the Olympic Mountains.

Ronald Olson's *The Quinault Indians*, most recently bound with his excellent *Adze, Canoe, and House Types of the Northwest Coast* [156], is one of the best Coast Salish ethnographies. Researched between 1925 and 1927, it describes traditional economic life, social structure, and religion in rewarding detail.

The now-extinct Chemakum of northwestern Puget Sound and the surviving Chemakum-speaking Quileute and Hoh of the Pacific coast of the Olympic Peninsula have both been the subject of several recent investigations. An ethnohistorical description of the Chemakum proper can be found in the Indian Claims Commission's study, "The Quileute Indians of Puget Sound" [208]. The Quileute have also been the subject of an ethnohistorical analysis by George Pettitt, "The Quileute of La Push, 1775–1945" [162]. Stationed in the village of La Push while in the Coast Guard during World War II, Pettitt gathered an extensive body of traditional information from the old people and did research in archives to produce his acculturation study. He found that their extremely isolated position, their successful maintenance of the traditional food economy, and many cultural parallels with White society permitted a gradual and relatively harmonious acculturation process. Pettitt was careful to point out, however, that while the Quileute have become very much like their White neighbors, they have remained and will remain a distinct group. The recent publication of Jay Powell and Vickie Jensen's *Quileute* [164] emphasizes this point. It is a well-illustrated, finely researched, and easily readable compilation of Quileute culture and language.

ALPHABETICAL LIST AND INDEX

*Denotes items suitable for secondary school students

[5]   Arima, Eugene Y. 1975. *A Report on a West Coast Whaling Canoe Reconstructed at Port Renfrew, B.C.* History and Archaeology, vol. 5. Ottawa: National Historic Parks and Sites Branch, Parks Canada, Department of Indian and Northern Affairs.   (48)

[6]   Arnold, Robert D., et al. 1976. *Alaska Native Land Claims.* Anchorage: Alaska Native Foundation. Distributed through American Indian Culture and Research Center, University of California, Los Angeles.   (19)

[7]   Averkieva, Julia P. 1966. *Slavery among the Indians of North America.* Revised ed., trans. G. R. Elliot. Victoria, B.C.: Victoria College. Originally published as *Rabstvo u Indietsev Severnoi Ameriki.* Moscow, 1941.   (14)

[8]   ———. 1971. "The Tlingit Indians." In *North American Indians in Historical Perspective,* ed. Eleanor Burke Leacock and Nancy Oestreich Lurie, pp. 317–42. New York: Random House.   (33)

[9]   Barbeau, Charles Marius. 1929. *Totem Poles of the Gitksan, Upper Skeena River, British Columbia*. National Museum of Canada Anthropological Series no. 12, Bulletin 61. Ottawa: F. A. Acland. Reprinted, Ottawa: National Museum of Man, 1973.   (20, 39)

[10]   ———. 1951. *Totem Poles*. 2 vols. National Museum of Canada Anthropological Series no. 30, Bulletin 119. Ottawa: National Museums of Canada.   (20)

[11]   ———. 1957. *Haida Carvers in Argillite*. National Museum of Canada Anthropological Series no. 38, Bulletin 139. Ottawa: National Museums of Canada. Reprinted, 1974.   (35)

[12]   ———. 1958. *Medicine-Men on the North Pacific Coast*. National Museum of Canada Anthropological Series 42, Bulletin 152. Ottawa: Department of Northern Affairs and National Resources, National Museums of Canada. Reprinted, 1973.   (30)

[13]   Barnett, Homer Garner. 1938. "The
Nature of the Potlatch." *American Anthropologist* 40:349–58.   (23)

[14]   ———. 1939. "Culture Element Distri-
bution Number 9: Gulf of Georgia
Salish." *Anthropological Records of the
University of California* 1:221–95.   (52)

[15]   ———. 1955. *The Coast Salish of British
Columbia.* University of Oregon Mono-
graphs, Studies in Anthropology, vol. 4.
Eugene: University of Oregon Press.   (52)

[16]   ———. 1957. *Indian Shakers: A Mes-
sianic Cult of the Pacific Northwest.*
Carbondale, Ill.: Southern Illinois University Press.   (55)

[17]   Benedict, Ruth Fulton. 1934. *Patterns of
Culture.* New York: Houghton Mifflin.
Reprinted, Boston: Houghton Mifflin,
1961.   (24)

[18]   Blackman, Margaret B. 1973. "The
Northern and Kaigani Haida: A Study
in Photographic Ethnohistory." Ph.D.
diss., Ohio State University.   (36)

[19] ———. 1973. "Totems to Tombstones: Culture Change as Viewed through the Haida Mortuary Complex, 1877– 1971." *Ethnology* 12:47–56.   (36)

[20] Boas, Franz. 1897. "The Social Organization and Secret Societies of the Kwakiutl Indians." In *Report of the United States National Museum for 1895,* pp. 311–738. Washington, D.C.: Government Printing Office. Reprinted, New York: Johnson, 1970; New York: Scholarly Reprints, 1976.   (42)

[21] ———. 1909. "The Kwakiutl of Vancouver Island." *Memoirs of the American Museum of Natural History* 8, part 2: 301–522. New York: American Museum of Natural History. Reprinted, New York: AMS, 1975.   (43)

[22] ———. 1916. *Tsimshian Mythology.* Thirty-first Annual Report of the United States Bureau of American Ethnology. Washington, D.C.: Government Printing Office. Reprinted, New York: Johnson, 1970.   (38)

[23]   ———. 1925. *Contributions to the Ethnology of the Kwakiutl.* Columbia University Contributions to Anthropology, vol. 3. New York: Columbia University Press. Reprinted, New York: AMS, 1969.   (43)

[24]   ———. 1927. *Primitive Art.* Oslo: Instituttet for Sammenlignende Kulturforskning by H. Aschehoug. Published the same year, Cambridge: Harvard University Press. Reprinted, New York: Dover, 1955.   (19)

[25]   ———. 1966. *Kwakiutl Ethnography,* ed. Helen Codere. Chicago: University of Chicago Press. Reprinted, 1975.   (43)

[26]   Borden, Charles E. 1975. *Origins and Development of Early Northwest Coast Culture to about 3,000 B.C.* Mercury Series, Archaeological Survey of Canada, Paper no. 45. Ottawa: National Museums of Canada.   (9)

[27]   ———. 1979. "Peopling and Early Cultures of the Pacific Northwest: A View from British Columbia, Canada." *Science* 203: 963–71.   (9)

[28] British Columbia Royal Commission on Indian Affairs. 1916. *Report of the Royal Commission on Indian Affairs for the Province of British Columbia*, 4 vols. Victoria, B.C.: Acme Press. (16)

[29]* Brown, Vinson, 1977. *Peoples of the Sea Wind: The Native Americans of the Pacific Coast.* New York: Macmillan. (7)

[30] Carlson, Roy L., ed. 1970. *Archaeology in British Columbia: New Discoveries. British Columbia Studies* 6–7, special issue. (10)

[31]* Carr, Emily. 1941. *Klee Wyck.* London and Toronto: Oxford University Press. Reprinted, Toronto: Farrar and Rinehart. 1942; Toronto: Clarke, Irwin, 1971. (7)

[32]* Carter, Anthony. 1966. *Somewhere Between.* Vancouver, B.C.: Agency Press. (42, 52)

[33]* ———. 1968. *This Is Haida.* Indian Heritage Series 2. Vancouver, B.C.: Agency Press. (35)

[34]* Carter, Anthony, and Chief Dan George. 1972. *Abundant Rivers.* Photographs, text, and design by Anthony Carter; ed. Chief Dan George. Indian Heritage Series 3. Saanichton, B.C.: Hancock House.   (40, 52)

[35]* Clutesi, George. 1969. *Potlatch.* Sidney, B.C.: Gray's Publishing Company.   (48)

[36] Codere, Helen. 1950. *Fighting with Property: A Study of Kwakiutl Potlatching and Warfare, 1792—1930.* Publications of the American Ethnological Society, no. 18. New York: J. J. Augustin.   (24, 43)

[37] ———. 1956. "The Amiable Side of Kwakiutl Life: The Potlatch and the Play Potlatch." *American Anthropologist* 58:334–51.   (24)

[38] ———. 1957. "Kwakiutl Society: Rank without Class." *American Anthropologist* 59:473–86.   (28)

[39] ———. 1961. "Kwakiutl." In *Perspectives in American Indian Culture Changes,* ed. Edward H. Spicer pp. 431–516. Chicago: Univeristy of Chicago Press. Reprinted, 1975. (44)

[40] Collins, June McCormick. 1974. *Valley of the Spirits: The Upper Skagit Indians of Western Washington.* Seattle: University of Washington Press. (57)

[41] ———. 1974. "Influence of White Contact on the Indians of Northern Puget Sound." United States Indian Claims Commission, American Indian Ethnohistory Series, ed. David Agee Horr. Indians of the Northwest, *Coast Salish and Western Washington Indians* 2:89–204. New York: Garland. (18, 57)

[42] ———. 1974. "A Study of Religious Change among the Skagit Indians of Washington." United States Indian Claims Commission, American Indian Ethnohistory Series, ed. David Agee Horr. Indians of the Northwest, *Coast Salish and Western Washington Indians* 4:619–763. New York: Garland. (18, 57)

[43]   Collison, William Henry. 1915. *In the Wake of the War Canoe: A Stirring Record of Forty Years' Successful Labour, Peril and Adventure amongst the Savage Indian Tribes of the Pacific Coast, and the Piratical Head-Hunting Haidas of the Queen Charlotte Islands, British Columbia.* London: Seeley, Service.   (29, 37)

[44]   Colson, Elizabeth. 1953. *The Makah Indians: A Study of an Indian Tribe in Modern American Society.* Minneapolis: University of Minnesota Press. Reprinted, Westport, Conn.: Greenwood, 1974.   (49)

[45]   Cook, James. 1784. *A Voyage to the Pacific Ocean Undertaken for Making Discoveries in the Northern Hemisphere to Determine the Position and Extent of the West Side of North America; Its Distance from Asia; and the Practicability of a Northern Passage to Europe. Performed under the Direction of Captains Cook, Clarke and Gore . . . in the Years 1776, 1777, 1778, 1779, and 1780.* Dublin: H. Chamberlain. Reprinted as *The Journals of Captain James Cook on His Voyages of Discovery,* ed. J. C. Beaglehole. Vol. 3, parts 1 and 2. *The*

Voyage of the Resolution and Discovery, 1776—1780. Cambridge: Published for the Hakluyt Society at the University Press, 1955. (46)

[46]   Croes, Dale R., ed. 1976. *The Excavation of Water-Saturated Archaeological Sites (Wet Sites) on the Northwest Coast of North America*. Mercury Series, Archaeological Survey of Canada, Paper no. 50. Ottawa: National Museums of Canada. (12)

[47]   Crosby, Thomas. 1907. *Among the An-Ko-Me-Nums or Flathead Tribes of Indians of the Pacific Coast*. Toronto: Briggs. (53)

[48]   Curtis, Edward Sheriff. 1907–30. *The North American Indians: Being a Series of Volumes Picturing and Describing the Indians of the United States and Alaska*, ed. Frederick Webb Hodge. 20 vols. Cambridge: Harvard University Press. (34)

[49]   ———. 1913. *The Salishan Tribes of the Coast*. Vol. 9 in *The North American Indians*. See [48]. Reprinted, New York: Johnson, 1970. (51)

[50]   ———. 1915. *The Kwakiutl.* Vol. 10 in
          The North American Indians. See [48].
          Reprinted, New York: Johnson,
          1970.   (41, 43)

[51]   ———. 1916. *The Nootka, The Haida.*
          Vol. 11 in *The North American Indians.*
          See [48]. Reprinted, New York:
          Johnson, 1970.   (47)

[52]   Cybulski, Jerome S. 1973. *The Gust Is-
          land Burial Shelter: Physical Anthropology.*
          Mercury Series, Archaeological Survey
          of Canada, Paper no. 9. Ottawa: Na-
          tional Museums of Canada. Bound with
          George F. MacDonald, *Haida Burial
          Practices: Three Archaeological Examples*
          [141].   (10)

[53]   ———. 1975. *Skeletal Variability in
          British Columbia Coastal Populations: A
          Descriptive and Comparative Assessment of
          Cranial Morphology.* Mercury Series, Ar-
          chaeological Survey of Canada, Paper
          no. 30. Ottawa: National Museums of
          Canada.   (10)

[54]   Davis, Robert Tyler. 1949. *Native Arts of
          the Pacific Northwest from the Rasmussen*

Collection of the Portland Art Museum. Stanford, Calif.: Stanford University Press. (20)

[55] De Laguna, Frederica. 1952. "Some Dynamic Forces in Tlingit Society." *Southwestern Journal of Anthropology* 8: 1–12. (33)

[56] ———. 1954. "Tlingit Ideas about the Individual." *Southwestern Journal of Anthropology* 10:172–91. (33)

[57] ———. 1960. *The Story of a Tlingit Community.* United States Bureau of American Ethnology Bulletin 172. Washington, D.C.: Government Printing Office. (9)

[58] ———. 1972. *Under Mount Saint Elias: The History and Culture of the Yakutat Tlingit.* 3 vols. Smithsonian Institution Contributions to Anthropology 7. Washington, D.C.: Smithsonian Institution Press. (33)

[59] De Laguna, Frederica, F. A. Riddell, D. F. McGeein, K. S. Lane, and J. A.

Freed. 1964. *Archaeology of the Yakutat Bay Area, Alaska.* United States Bureau of American Ethnology Bulletin 192. Washington, D.C.: Government Printing Office.   (9)

[60]   Densmore, Frances. 1939. *Nootka and Quileute Music.* United States Bureau of American Ethnology Bulletin 124. Washington, D.C.: Government Printing Office. Reprinted, New York: DaCapo, 1972.   (49)

[61]   ———. 1943. *Music of the Indians of British Columbia.* United States Bureau of American Ethnology Bulletin 136. Washington, D.C.: Government Printing Office. Reprinted, New York: DaCapo, 1972.   (5)

[62]   Dockstader, Frederick J. 1961. *Indian Art in America: The Arts and Crafts of the North American Indian.* Greenwich, Conn.: New York Graphic Society. New ed., 1966.   (21)

[63]   Donald, Leland, and Donald H. Mitchell. 1975. "Some Correlates of Local Group

Rank among the Southern Kwakiutl."
Ethnology 14:325–46. (26)

[64] Drucker, Philip. 1939. "Rank, Wealth and Kinship in Northwest Coast Society." *American Anthropologist* 41:55–65. (28)

[65] ———. 1940. "Kwakiutl Dancing Societies." *Anthropological Records of the University of California* 2(6):201–30. (41)

[66] ———. 1943. *Archaeological Survey of the Northern Northwest Coast.* United States Bureau of American Ethnology Bulletin 133, pp. 17–132. Washington, D.C.: Government Printing Office. (9)

[67] ———. 1950. "Culture Element Distribution Number 26: Northwest Coast." *Anthropological Records of the University of California* 9(3):157–294. (x, 41)

[68] ———. 1951. *The Northern and Central Nootkan Tribes.* United States Bureau of American Ethnology Bulletin 144. Washington, D.C.: Government Printing Office. (48)

[69]   ———. 1955. *Indians of the Northwest Coast*. Garden City, N.Y.: Natural History Press.   (5)

[70]   ———. 1955. "Sources of Northwest Coast Culture." In *New Interpretations of Aboriginal American Culture History*, ed. Betty J. Meggars, pp. 59–82. Washington, D.C.: Anthropological Society of Washington.   (x, 5)

[71]   ———. 1958. *The Native Brotherhoods: Modern Intertribal Organization on the Northwest Coast*. United States Bureau of American Ethnology Bulletin 168. Washington, D.C.: Government Printing Office.   (16)

[72]   ———. 1965. *Cultures of the North Pacific Coast*. San Francisco: Chandler.   (6)

[73]   ——— and Robert F. Heizer. 1967. *To Make My Name Good: A Reexamination of the Southern Kwakiutl Potlatch*. Berkeley: University of California Press.   (25)

[74]   Duff, Wilson. 1952. *The Upper Stalo Indians of the Fraser Valley, British Columbia*.

Anthropology in British Columbia, Memoir 1. Victoria, B.C.: British Columbia Provincial Museum of Natural History and Anthropology. Reprinted by the museum, 1973. (53)

[75] ———. 1964. "Contributions of Marius Barbeau to West Coast Ethnology." *Anthropologica* 6:63–96. (37)

[76]* ———. 1964. *The Indian History of British Columbia.* Vol. 1. *The Impact of the White Man.* Anthropology in British Columbia, Memoir 5. Victoria, B.C.: British Columbia Provincial Museum of Natural History and Anthropology. (13)

[77] ———. 1975. *Images Stone B.C.: Thirty Centuries of Northwest Coast Indian Sculpture.* Seattle: University of Washington Press. (13)

[78] ———, ed. 1959. *Histories, Territories and Laws of the Kitwancool.* Anthropology in British Columbia, Memoir 4. Victoria, B.C.: British Columbia Provincial Museum of Natural History and Anthropology. (39)

[79]   Duff, Wilson, Bill Holm, and Bill Reid. 1967. *Arts of the Raven: Masterworks by the Northwest Coast Indian. An Exhibition in Honour of the One Hundredth Anniversary of Canadian Confederation.* Catalog text by Wilson Duff with contributory articles by Bill Holm and Bill Reid. Vancouver, B.C.: Vancouver Art Gallery.   (22)

[80]   Duff, Wilson, and Michael Kew. 1958. "Anthony Island, a Home of the Haidas." *Annual Report of the Provincial Museum of British Columbia,* pp. 37–64.   (35)

[81]*   Durham, Bill. 1960. *Indian Canoes of the Northwest Coast.* Seattle: Copper Canoe Press.   (6)

[82]   Durlach, Theresa Mayer. 1928. *The Relationship Systems of the Tlingit, Haida and Tsimshian.* Publications of the American Ethnological Society 11. New York: Published for the American Ethnological Society by G. E. Stechert.   (30)

[83]   Eells, Myron. 1887. "The Twana, Chemakum and Klallum Indians of

Washington Territory." *Annual Report of the Smithsonian Institution for 1887,* part 1:605–81. Reprinted, Seattle: Shorey Publications, 1971.   (55)

[84] Elmendorf, William W. 1960. *The Structure of Twana Culture. Research Studies, Washington State University* 28(3), suppl. 2. Pullman, Wash.: Washington State University Press. Reprinted by United States Indian Claims Commission, American Indian Ethnohistory Series, Indians of the Northwest, *Coast Salish and Western Washington Indians* 4:27–566. New York: Garland, 1974.   (18, 58)

[85] Emmons, George Thornton. 1903. "The Basketry of the Tlingit." *Memoirs of the American Museum of Natural History* 3, part 2:229–77.   (19, 31)

[86] Emmons, George Thornton, and Franz Boas. 1907. "The Chilkat Blanket, with Notes on Blanket Designs." *Memoirs of the American Museum of Natural History* 3, part 4:329–400.   (19, 31)

[87]   Feder, Norman. 1971. *American Indian Art*. New York: Abrams.   (22)

[88]   Fields, D. B., and W. T. Stanbury. 1970. *The Economic Impact of the Public Sector upon the Indians of British Columbia: A Report Submitted to the Department of Indian Affairs and Northern Development*. Vancouver, B.C.: University of British Columbia Press.   (17, 54)

[89]   Fladmark, Knut R. 1975. *A Paleoecological Model for Northwest Coast Prehistory*. Mercury Series, Archaeological Survey of Canada, Paper no. 43. Ottawa: National Museums of Canada.   (9)

[90]*   Flucke, A. F., and A. E. Pickford. 1952. *Haida*. British Columbia Heritage Series 1, vol. 4. Victoria, B.C.: A. Sutton.   (35)

[91]*   ———. 1965. *Coast Salish*. British Columbia Heritage Series 1, vol. 2. Victoria, B.C.: A. Sutton.   (52)

[92]*   ———. 1966. *Introduction to Our Native Peoples*. British Columbia Heritage

Series 1, vol. 1. Victoria, B.C.: A. Sutton. (8)

[93]* ———. 1966. *Kwakiutl.* British Columbia Heritage Series 1, vol. 7. Victoria, B.C.: A. Sutton. (44)

[94]* ———. 1966. *Nootka.* British Columbia Heritage Series 1, vol. 5. Victoria, B.C.: A. Sutton. (48)

[95]* ———. 1966. *Tsimshian.* British Columbia Heritage Series 1, vol. 6. Victoria, B.C.: A. Sutton. (36)

[96] Garfield, Viola Edmundson. 1939. *Tsimshian Clan and Society.* University of Washington Publications in Anthropology 7(3). Seattle: University of Washington Press. (38)

[97] Garfield, Viola Edmundson, and Linn Argyle Forrest. 1948. *The Wolf and the Raven: Totem Poles of Southeastern Alaska.* Seattle: University of Washington Press. Rev. ed., 1973. (20)

[98]   Garfield, Viola Edmundson, Paul Stover Wingert, and Charles Marius Barbeau. 1951. *The Tsimshian: Their Arts and Music*. Publications of the American Ethnological Society 18. New York: Published for the American Ethnological Society by J. J. Augustin.   (38)

[99]   Garfield, Viola Edmundson, and Paul Stover Wingert. 1966. *The Tsimshian Indians and Their Arts*. Seattle: University of Washington Press.   (38)

[100]   Gillis, Alix Jane. 1974. "History of the Neah Bay Agency." United States Indian Claims Commission, American Indian Ethnohistory Series, Indians of the Northwest, *Coast Salish and Western Washington Indians*, 3:91–115. New York: Garland.   (18, 49)

[101]   Goddard, Pliny Earle. 1924. *Indians of the Northwest Coast*. New York: American Museum of Natural History. Reprinted, 1934; new ed., 1945; second reprinting, New York: Cooper Square Publishers, 1972.   (4)

[102] Goldman, Irving. 1975. *The Mouth of Heaven: An Introduction to Kwakiutl Religious Thought.* New York: John Wiley.   (28)

[103] Grumet, Robert Steven. 1975. "Changes in Coast Tsimshian Redistributive Activities in the Fort Simpson Region of British Columbia, 1788–1862." *Ethnohistory* 22(4):294–318.   (39)

[104] Gunther, Erna. 1927. *Klallam Ethnography.* University of Washington Publications in Anthropology 1, no. 5. Seattle: University of Washington Press.   (55)

[105] ———. 1928. *A Further Analysis of the First Salmon Ceremony.* University of Washington Publications in Anthropology 2, no. 5. Seattle: University of Washington Press.   (6)

[106] ———. 1966. *Art in the Life of the Northwest Coast Indian, with a Catalogue of the Rasmussen Collection of Northwest Indian Art at the Portland Museum.* Portland: Portland Art Museum.   (21)

[107]   ———. 1972. *Indian Life on the Northwest Coast of North America as Seen by the Early Explorers and Fur Traders during the Last Decades of the Eighteenth Century.* Chicago: University of Chicago Press. Reprinted,1975.   (14)

[108]   ———. 1973. *Ethnobotany of Western Washington: The Knowledge and Use of Indigenous Plants by Native Americans.* Revised ed., Seattle: University of Washington Press. Originally published in 1945 as *Ethnobotany of Western Washington.* University of Washington Publications in Anthropology 10:1–61.   (55)

[109]   Haeberlin, Hermann K, and Erna Gunther. 1930. *Indians of Puget Sound.* University of Washington Publications in Anthropology 4 no. 1. Seattle: University of Washington Press.   (56)

[110]   Halpin, Marjorie Myers. 1973. "The Tsimshian Crest System: A Study Based on Museum Specimens and the Marius Barbeau and William Beynon Field Notes." Ph.D. diss., University of British Columbia.   (38)

[111] ———. 1978. "William Beynon,
       Tsimshian, 1888–1958." *In American
       Indian Intellectuals: 1976 Proceedings of
       the American Ethnological Society*, ed.
       Margot Liberty, pp. 141–58. St. Paul,
       Minn.: West Publishing Company.   (37)

[112] Harris, Kenneth B., and Frances
       Robinson. 1974. *Visitors Who Never Left:
       The Origin of the People of Damelahamid*.
       Vancouver, B.C.: University of British
       Columbia Press.   (40)

[113] Hawthorn, Audrey. 1967. *Art of the
       Kwakiutl Indians and Other Northwest
       Coast Tribes*. Seattle: University of Wash-
       ington Press.   (21)

[114] Hawthorn, Harry Betram, Cyril S.
       Belshaw, and Samuel M. Jamieson.
       1958. *The Indians of British Columbia: A
       Study of Contemporary Social Adjustment*.
       Berkeley: University of California
       Press.   (17)

[115]* Hays, H. R. 1975. *Children of the Raven:
       The Seven Indian Nations of the Northwest
       Coast*. New York: McGraw-Hill.   (7, 13)

[116]*   Hill, Beth, and Ray Hill. 1974. *Indian Petroglyphs of the Pacific Northwest.* Saanichton, B.C.: Hancock House.   (13)

[117]   Holm. Bill. 1965. *Northwest Coast Indian Art: An Analysis of Form.* Thomas Burke Memorial Washington State Museum, Monograph no. 1. Seattle: University of Washington Press.   (21)

[118]   Holm, Bill, and William Reid. 1975. *Form and Freedom.* Seattle: University of Washington Press.   (22, 28)

[119]   Inverarity, Robert Bruce. 1950. *Art of the Northwest Coast Indians.* Berkeley: University of California Press.   (21)

[120]   Jacobsen, Johan Adrian. 1977. *Alaskan Voyage, 1881–1883: An Expedition to the Northwest Coast of America,* trans. Erna Gunther. Chicago: University of Chicago Press.   (14)

[121]   Jenness, Diamond. 1973. *The Faith of a Coast Salish Indian.* Bound with Wayne Suttles, *Katzie Ethnographic Notes,* ed.

Wilson Duff. Victoria, B.C.: British Columbia Provincial Museum of Natural History and Anthropology. Originally published in 1955 in *Anthropology in British Columbia,* Memoir 3 of the museum. (53)

[122] Jewitt, John R. 1824. *The Adventures and Sufferings of John R. Jewitt, Captive among the Nootka, 1803–05.* Edinburgh: A. Constable. Reprinted, Toronto: McClelland and Stewart, 1974. (46)

[123] Jilek, Wolfgang G. 1974. *Salish Indian Mental Health and Culture Change: Psychohygienic and Therapeutic Aspects of the Guardian Spirit Ceremonial.* Toronto: Holt, Rinehart and Winston of Canada. (54)

[124] Jones, Joan Meagan. 1968. *Northwest Coast Basketry and Culture Change.* Research Report no. 1. Thomas Burke Memorial Washington State Museum. Seattle: University of Washington Press. (21)

[125] Jones, Livingston French. 1914. *A Study of the Thlingets of Alaska.* New York:

Fleming H. Revell Company. Reprinted, New York: Johnson, 1970.   (31)

[126]   Kane, Paul. 1859. *Wanderings of an Artist among the Indians of North America from Canada to Vancouver's Island and Oregon through the Hudson's Bay Company's Territory and Back Again.* Toronto: Longman, Brown, Green and Roberts. Rev. ed., 1925. Reprinted, Edmonton, Alb.: Hurtig Publishers, 1968, 1974.   (50)

[127]*   Keithahn, Edward Linnaeus. 1945. *Monuments in Cedar: The Authentic Story of the Totem Pole.* Ketchikan, Alaska: R. Anderson. Rev. ed., New York: Bonanza Books, 1963.   (30)

[128]*   Kew, Della, and Pliny Earle Goddard. 1974. *Indian Art and Culture of the Northwest Coast.* Saanichton, B.C.: Hancock House.   (4)

[129]*   Kirk, Ruth, and Richard D. Daugherty. 1974. *Hunters of the Whale: An Adventure in Northwest Coast Archaeology.* New York: Morrow.   (12)

[130] Klein, Laura Frances. 1975. "Tlingit Women and Town Politics." Ph.D. diss., New York University. (34)

[131] Kobrinsky, Vernon H. 1976. "Dynamics of the Fort Rupert Class Struggle: Fighting with Property Vertically Revisited." In *Papers in Honour of Harry Hawthorn,* ed. Vernon Serl and Herbert C. Taylor, pp. 32–59. Bellingham, Wash.: Western Washington State College. (28)

[132] Koppert, Vincent Aloysius. 1930. *Contributions to Clayoquot Ethnology.* Washington, D.C.: Catholic University of America. (48)

[133] Krause, Aurel. 1885. *Die Tlinkit-Indianer.* Jena: H. Costenoble. Republished as *The Tlingit Indians: Results of a Trip to the Northwest Coast of America and the Bering Straits,* trans. Erna Gunther. Seattle: Published for the American Ethnological Society by the University of Washington Press, 1956. (30)

[134]   La Violette, Forrest E. 1961. *The Struggle for Survival: Indian Cultures and the
Protestant Ethnic in British Columbia.* Toronto: University of Toronto Press.
Rev. ed., 1973.   (15)

[135]   Lemert, Edwin McCarthy. 1954. "Alco-
hol and the Northwest Coast Indians."
*University of California Publications in
Culture and Society* 2(6):303–406.   (16)

[136]   Levine, Robert, ed. 1976. *Native Languages and Culture. Sound Heritage* 4(3–
4), special issue.   (16)

[137]   Lewis, Claudia. 1970. *Indian Families of
the Northwest Coast.* Chicago: University
of Chicago Press.   (53)

[138]   Lopatin, Ivan Alexis. 1945. *Social Life
and Religion of the Indians in Kitimat,
British Columbia.* University of Southern
California Social Science Series no. 26.
Los Angeles: University of Southern
California.   (41)

[139] McClellen, Catharine. 1954. "The Interrelationships of Social Structure with Northern Tlingit Ceremonialism." *Southwestern Journal of Anthropology* 10:75–96. (33)

[140] MacDonald, George F. 1973. *Haida Burial Practices: Three Archaeological Examples.* Mercury Series, Archaeological Survey of Canada, Paper no. 9. Ottawa: National Museums of Canada. Bound with Jerome S. Cybulski, *The Gust Island Burial Shelter: Physical Anthropology* [53]. (11)

[141]* MacDonald, George F. et al., 1972. *'KSAN: Breath of Our Grandfathers.* Ottawa: National Museums of Canada. (40)

[142] McFeat, Thomas R., ed. 1966. *Indians of the North Pacific Coast.* Toronto: McClelland and Stewart. New ed., Seattle: University of Washington Press, 1967. (5)

[143] McIlwraith, Thomas F. 1948. *The Bella Coola Indians.* 2 vols. Toronto: University of Toronto Press. (45)

[144]*   ———. 1953. *Bella Coola*. British Co-
lumbia Heritage Series, Our Native
People, ser. 1, vol. 10. Victoria, B.C.: A.
Sutton.   (45)

[145]   Macnair, Peter L. 1973–74. "Kwakiutl
Winter Dances: A Reenactment," and
"Potlatch at Alert Bay." *Artscanada*
184–87:94–118.   (45)

[146]*   Meade, Edward. 1971. *Indian Rock
Carvings of the Pacific Northwest*. Sidney,
B.C.: Gray's Publishing Company.   (12)

[147]*   Miller, Polly, and Leon Gordon Miller.
1967. *The Lost Heritage of Alaska: The
Adventure and Art of the Alaskan Coastal
Indians*. Cleveland: World.   (14)

[148]   Mitchell, Donald H. 1971. *Archaeology of
the Gulf of Georgia Area: A Natural Region and Its Culture Types. Syesis* 4, suppl.
1:1–228.   (11)

[149]   Moziño, José Mariano. 1970. *Noticias de
Nutka: An Account of Nootka Sound in*

1792, trans. and ed. Iris Higbie Wilson. Seattle: University of Washington Press.   (46)

[150]   Murdock, George Peter. 1934. "Kinship and Social Behavior among the Haida." *American Anthropologist* 36:355–85.   (34)

[151]   ———. 1936. "Rank and Potlatch among the Haida," *Yale University Publications in Anthropology* 13:1–20.   (35)

[152]   Murdock, George Peter, and Timothy O'Leary. 1975. "Northwest Coast." In *Ethnographic Bibliography of North America*, 3:1–64. 4th ed. New Haven: Human Relations Area File Press.   (ix)

[153]   Niblack, Albert P. 1890. "The Coast Indians of Southern Alaska and Northern British Columbia." "In *Annual Report of the United States National Museum for 1888*, pp. 225–386. Washington, D.C.: United States National Museum. Reprinted, New York: Johnson, 1970.   (29)

[154]   Nowell, Charles James. 1941. *Smoke from Their Fires: The Life of a Kwakiutl*

Chief by Clellan S. Ford. New Haven, Conn.: Yale University Press, New ed., Hamden, Conn.: Archon Books, 1968.   (43)

[155]   Oberg, Kalervo. 1973. *The Social Economy of the Tlingit Indians.* Seattle: University of Washington Press.   (32)

[156]   Olson, Ronald Le Roy. 1927–36. *The Quinault Indians* and *Adze, Canoe, and House Types of the Northwest Coast.* University of Washington Publications in Anthropology 2 (1927) and 6, no. 1 (1936). Seattle: University of Washington Press. Reprinted together as a monograph, 1967.   (59)

[157]   ———. 1940. "The Social Organization of the Haisla." *Anthropological Records of the University of California* 2(5): 169–200.   (41)

[158]   ———. 1954. "Social Life of the Owikeno Kwakiutl." *Anthropological Records of the University of California* 14(3):213–59.   (44)

[159] ———. 1955. "Notes on the Bella Bella Kwakiutl." *Anthropological Records of the University of California* 14(5):319–48. (41)

[160] ———. 1967. "Social Structure and Social Life of the Tlingit in Alaska." *Anthropological Records of the University of California* 26. Reprinted, Millwood, N.Y.: Kraus, 1976. (32)

[161] Paul, Frances. 1944. *The Spruce Root Basketry of the Tlingit.* Lawrence, Kans.: Haskell Institute. (32)

[162] Pettitt, George Albert. 1950. "The Quileute of La Push, 1775–1945." *Anthropological Records of the University of California* 14(1):1–128. (59)

[163] Piddocke, Stuart M. 1965. "The Potlatch System of the Southern Kwakiutl: A New Perspective." *Southwestern Journal of Anthropology* 21:244–64. (25)

[164]* Powell, Jay, and Vickie Jensen. 1976. *Quileute: An Introduction to the Indians of La Push.* Seattle: University of Washington Press. (59)

[165]* Reid, William, and Adelaide de Menil. 1971. *Out of Silence,* New York: Outerbridge and Dienstfrey. Published for the Amon Carter Museum, Fort Worth, Texas.   (22)

[166]   Riley, Carroll L. 1974. "Investigations and Analysis of the Puget Sound Indians." United States Indian Claims Commission, American Indian Ethnohistory Series, Indians of the Northwest, *Coast Salish and Western Washington Indians* 2:27–87. New York: Garland.   (18, 56)

[167]   Roberts, Helen H., and Morris Swadesh. 1955. "Songs of the Nootka Indians of Western Vancouver Island." In *Transactions of the American Philosophical Society* 45:199–327. Philadelphia: American Philosophical Society.   (47)

[168]   Rohner, Ronald P. 1967. *The People of Gilford: A Contemporary Kwakiutl Village.* National Museums of Canada Bulletin 225. Ottawa: Queen's Printer.   (44)

[169]   ———. 1969. *The Ethnography of Franz Boas: Letters and Diaries of Franz Boas*

Written on the Northwest Coast from 1886 to 1931. Chicago: University of Chicago Press.   (14)

[170]   Rohner, Ronald P., and Evelyn C. Rohner. 1970. *The Kwakiutl: Indians of British Columbia*. New York: Holt, Rinehard and Winston.   (44)

[171]   Rosman, Abraham, and Paula Rubel. 1971. *Feasting with Mine Enemy: Rank and Exchange among Northwest Coast Societies*. New York: Columbia University Press.   (27)

[172]   ———. 1972. "The Potlatch: A Structural Analysis." *American Anthropologist* 74:658–71.   (27)

[173]   Ruyle, Eugene E. 1973. "Slavery, Surplus and Stratification on the Northwest Coast: The Ethnoenergetics of an Incipient Stratification System." *Current Anthropology 14:603–*31.   (27)

[174]* Salisbury, Oliver M. 1962. *The Customs and Legends of the Thlinget Indians of Alaska.* New York: Bonanza. Originally published as *Quoth the Raven: A Little Journey into the Primitive.* Seattle: Superior Publishing Company, 1962.   (32)

[175]   Sapir, Edward. 1915. "A Sketch of the Social Organization of the Nass River Indians." *Museum Bulletin of the Canadian Department of Mines* 19:1–30.   (37)

[176]* Siebert, Erna, and Werner Forman. 1967. *North American Indian Art: Masks, Amulets, Wood Carvings and Ceremonial Dress from the Northwest Coast,* trans. Philippa Heniges; originally published in German. London: Paul Hamlyn.   (22)

[177]   Simonsen, Bjorn O. 1973. *Archaeological Investigations in the Hecate Strait– Milbanke Sound Area of British Columbia.* Mercury Series, Archaeological Survey of Canada, Paper no. 13. Ottawa: National Museums of Canada.   (11)

[178]   Smith, Harlan Ingersoll. 1928. "Materia Medica of the Bella Coola and

Neighbouring Tribes of British Columbia." National Museum of Canada Bulletin 56:47–68 Ottawa: National Museums of Canada. (45)

[179] Smith, Marian Wesley. 1940. *The Puyallup-Nisqually.* Columbia University Contributions to Anthropology 32. Reprinted, New York: AMS, 1969. (56)

[180] ———, ed. 1949. *Indians of the Urban Northwest.* Columbia University Contributions to Anthropology 36. Reprinted, New York: AMS, 1969. (51)

[181] Smyly, John, and Carolyn Smyly. 1975. *The Totem Poles of Skedans.* Seattle: University of Washington Press. Originally published in 1973 as *Those Born at Koona.* Saanichton, B.C.: Hancock House. (36)

[182] Snyder, Sally. 1975. "Quest for the Sacred in Northern Puget Sound: An Interpretation of Potlatch." *Ethnology* 14(2):149–61. (27)

[183]   Spradley, James Philip, ed. *Guests Never Leave Hungry: The Autobiography of James Sewid, a Kwakiutl Indian.* New Haven, Conn.: Yale University Press. New ed., Montreal and London: McGill–Queen's University Press, 1972.   (44)

[184]   Sproat, Gilbert Malcom. 1868. *Scenes and Studies of Savage Life.* London: Smith, Elder.   (47)

[185]*   Steltzer, Ulli. 1976. *Indian Artists at Work.* Seattle: University of Washington Press. New ed., Vancouver. B.C,: J. J. Douglas, 1977.   (22)

[186]   Stern, Bernhard Joseph. 1934. *The Lummi Indians of Northwest Washington.* Columbia University Contributions to Anthropology 17. Reprinted, New York: AMS, 1969.   (55)

[187]*   Stewart, Hilary. 1973. *Artifacts of the Northwest Coast Indians.* Saanichton, B.C.: Hancock House.   (6)

[188]*   ———. 1977. *Indian Fishing: Early Methods on the Northwest Coast*. Seattle: University of Washington Press.   (5)

[189]   Stott, Margaret A. 1975. *Bella Coola Ceremony and Art*. Mercury Series, Ethnology Division, Paper no. 21. Ottawa: National Museums of Canada.   (45)

[190]   Stuart, Wendy Bross. 1972. *Gambling Music of the Coast Salish Indians*. Mercury Series, Ethnology Division, Paper no. 3. Ottawa: National Museums of Canada.   (51)

[191]   Suttles, Wayne P. 1954. "Post-Contact Culture Changes among the Lummi Indians." *British Columbia Historical Quarterly* 18:29–102.   (56)

[192]   ———. 1960. "Affinal Ties, Subsistence, and Prestige among the Coast Salish." *American Anthropologist* 62:296–305.   (25)

[193]   ———. 1962. "Variation in Habitat and Culture on the Northwest Coast." *Akten des 34. Internationalen Amerikanistenkon-*

gresses, Wein, 1960, pp. 522–37. Vienna: International Congress of Americanists.   (26)

[194]   ———. 1968. "Coping with Abundance: Subsistence on the Northwest Coast." In *Man the Hunter,* ed. Richard Borshay Lee and Irven De Vore, pp. 56–69. Chicago: Aldine.   (26)

[195]   ———. 1972. "On the Cultural Trail of the Sasquatch." *Northwest Anthropological Research Notes* 6(1):65–90.   (51)

[196]   ———. 1973. *Katzie Ethnographic Notes.* Bound with Diamond Jenness, *The Faith of a Coast Salish Indian.* Victoria, B.C.: British Columbia Provincial Museum of Natural History and Anthropology. Originally published in 1955 in *Anthropology in British Columbia,* Memoir 2, British Columbia Provincial Museum.   (53)

[197]   ———. 1974. "Economic Life of the Coast Salish of Haro and Rosario Straits." United States Indian Claims Commission, American Indian

Ethnohistory Series, Indians of the Northwest, *Coast Salish and Western Washington Indians* 1:41–570. New York: Garland.　　　　　(18, 56)

[198] Swadesh, Morris. 1948. "Motivations in Nootka Warfare." *Southwestern Journal of Anthropology* 4:76–93.　　　　　(47)

[199] Swan, James Gilchrist. 1857. *The Northwest Coast: or, Three Years Residence in Washington Territory.* New York: Harper. Reprinted, Seattle: University of Washington Press, 1972.　　　　　(58)

[200] ———. 1869. *The Indians of Cape Flattery, at the Entrance to the Strait of Fuca, Washington Territory.* Smithsonian Institution Contributions to Knowledge 16. Washington, D.C.: Smithsonian Institution. Reprinted, Seattle: Shorey Publications, 1960.　　　　　(48)

[201] Swanton, John Reed. 1905. *Contributions to the Ethnology of the Haida.* Memoirs of the American Museum of Natural History 8, part 1. New York:

E. E. Stechert. Reprinted, New York, AMS, 1975.   (34)

[202]   ———. 1908. "Social Condition, Beliefs and Linguistic Relationship of the Tlingit Indians." In *Twenty-sixth Annual Report of the United States Bureau of American Ethnology, 1904–5*, pp. 391–485. Washington, D.C.: Government Printing Office.   (31)

[203]   Taylor, Herbert C., Jr. 1974. "Anthropological Investigation of the Medicine Creek Tribes." United States Indian Claims Commission, American Indian Ethnohistory Series, Indians of the Northwest, *Coast Salish and Western Washington Indians* 2:401–73. New York: Garland.   (18, 58)

[204]   ———. 1974. "Anthropological Investigation of the Makah Indians." United States Indian Claims Commission, American Indian Ethnohistory Series, Indians of the Northwest, *Coast Salish and Western Washington Indians* 3:27–89. New York: Garland.   (18, 49)

[205]* Turner, Nancy J. 1975. *Food Plants of British Columbia Indians: Part 1. Coastal Peoples.* British Columbia Provincial Museum of Natural History and Anthropology Handbook 34. Victoria, B.C.: British Columbia Provincial Museum. (5, 55)

[206] Tweddell, Colin E. 1974. "Historical and Ethnological Study of the Snohomish Indian People." United States Indian Claims Commission, American Indian Ethnohistory Series, ed. David Agee Horr. Indians of the Northwest, *Coast Salish and Western Washington Indians* 2:475–694. New York: Garland. (18, 57)

[207]* Underhill, Ruth M. 1945. *Indians of the Pacific Northwest.* Riverside, Calif.: Sherman Institute Press. Reprinted, Washington, D.C.: Department of the Interior, Bureau of Indian Affairs, Branch of Education; New York, AMS, 1978. (54)

[208] United States Indian Claims Commission. 1974. "The Quileute Indians of

Puget Sound." American Indian Ethnohistory Series, ed. David Agee Horr. Indians of the Northwest, *Coast Salish and Western Washington Indians* 2:205–400. New York: Garland.   (18, 59)

[209]   Usher, Jean. 1974. *William Duncan of Metlakatla: A Victorian Missionary in British Columbia.* National Museum of Man Publications in History 5. Ottawa: National Museums of Canada.   (38)

[210]   Van den Brink, J. H. 1974. *The Haida Indians: Cultural Change Mainly between 1876–1970.* Monographs and Theoretical Studies in Sociology and Anthropology in Honour of Nels Anderson, Publication 8. Leiden: E. J. Brill.   (36)

[211]   Vayda, Andrew Peter. 1961. "A Reexamination of Northwest Coast Economic Systems." *Transactions of the New York Academy of Sciences* 23(7)):618–24.   (25)

[212]   Waterman, Thomas Talbot. 1920. *The Whaling Equipment of the Makah Indians.* University of Washington Publications

in Anthropology 1(2). Seattle: University of Washington Press. (49)

[213] ———. 1973. *Notes on the Ethnology of the Indians of Puget Sound.* Indian Notes and Monographs, Miscellaneous Series no. 59. New York: Museum of American Indian, Heye Foundation. (55)

[214] Waterman, Thomas Talbot, and G. Coffin. 1920. *Types of Canoes on Puget Sound.* Indian Notes and Monographs no. 5. New York: Museum of the American Indian, Heye Foundation. (54)

[215] Waterman, Thomas Talbot, and Ruth Griener. 1921. *Indian Homes of Puget Sound.* Indian Notes and Monographs no. 9. New York: Museum of the American Indian, Heye Foundation. (54)

[216] Weinberg, Daniela. 1965. "Models of Southern Kwakiutl Social Organization." *Yearbook of the Society for General Systems Research* 10:169–81. Reprinted in *Cultural Ecology,* ed. Bruce Cox, pp. 227–53. Toronto: McClelland and Stewart, 1973. (26)

[217]   Wellcome, Henry Solomon. 1887. *The Story of Metlakahtla*. New York: Saxon.   (37)

[218]*   Wherry, Joseph H. 1964. *Totem Pole Indians*. New York: Funk and Wagnalls. Reprinted, New York: Crowell, 1974   (7)

[219]   Wike, Joyce Annabel. 1951. "The Effect of the Maritime Fur Trade on Northwest Coast Indian Society." Ph.D. diss., Columbia University.   (14)

[220]   Wingert, Paul Stover. 1949. *American Indian Sculpture: A Study of the Northwest Coast*. New York: J. J. Augustin. Reprinted, New York: Hacker Art Books, 1976.   (21)

[221]   Wolcott, Harry F. 1967. *A Kwakiutl Village and School*. New York: Holt, Rinehart and Winston.   (45)

[222]*   Woodcock, George. 1977. *Peoples of the Coast: The Indians of the Pacific Northwest*. Bloomington: Indiana University Press.   (8, 25)

The Newberry Library
Center for the History of the American Indian
Founding Director: D'Arcy McNickle
Director: Francis Jennings

Established in 1972 by the Newberry Library, in conjunction with the Committee on Institutional Cooperation of eleven midwestern universities, the Center makes the resources of one of America's foremost research libraries in the Humanities available to those interested in improving the quality and effectiveness of teaching American Indian history. The Newberry's collections include some 100,000 volumes on the history of the American Indian and offer specialized resources for studying historical aspects of Indian-White relations and Indian linguistics. The Center also assists Native Americans engaged in writing tribal histories and developing educational materials.

ADVISORY COMMITTEE

Chairman: Alfonso Ortiz
University of New Mexico

Robert F. Berkhofer
University of Michigan

Robert V. Dumont, Jr.
Native American Educational Services/Antioch College;
Fort Peck Reservation

Raymond D. Fogelson
University of Chicago

William T. Hagan
State University of New York College, Fredonia

Nancy O. Lurie
Milwaukee Public Museum

Cheryl Metoyer-Duran
University of California, Los Angeles

N. Scott Momaday
Stanford University

Father Peter J. Powell
St. Augustine Indian Center

Father Paul Prucha, s.j.
Marquette University

Faith Smith
Native American Educational Services/Antioch College;
Chicago

Sol Tax
University of Chicago

Robert K. Thomas
Wayne State University

Robert M. Utley
Advisory Council on Historical Preservation; Washington, D.C.

Antoinette McNickle Vogel
Gaithersburg, MD.

Dave Warren
Institute of American Indian Arts

Wilcomb E. Washburn
Smithsonian Institution